Dawn of a New Day

Dawn of a New Day

The Timing of Christ's Return — And Why It Matters

*A Collection of Original Articles
On End Times Theology*

Nelson Walters

With

Bob Brown

Copyright 2019 by Nelson Walters

Unless otherwise noted, all Scripture quotations are taken from the New American Standard Bible® marked *NASB*, Copyright 1960, 1962, 1963, 1968, 1971, 1972, 1973, 1975, 1977, 1995 by The Lockman Foundation. Used by permission.

Scripture quotations marked "LXX" are from the Septuagint: Translation by Sir Lancelot C. L. Brenton, 1851, Public Domain.

All rights reserved solely by the author. No part of this book may be reproduced, stored in a retrieval system, or transmitted, in any form or by any means, electronic, mechanical, photocopying, recording, or otherwise, without the prior written permission of the author.

Because of the dynamic nature of the Internet, any web addresses or links contained in this book may have changed since publication and may no longer be valid.

Special thanks to Sandra Haas for her help in re-formatting video transcripts used in various articles in this book.

Ready For Jesus Publications (Wilmington, NC, 2018)

ISBN - 9781070991276

Contents

Article One 1
  Will Everything Just Pan Out?

Article Two..9
  The Rapture Civil War

Article Three 17
  Will Christians Face the Great Tribulation?

Article Four 35
  Why Does God Permit Great Tribulation?

Article Five 43
  Is Rapture the Best Word to Use?

Article Six 51
  Let No One Deceive You

Article Seven...61
  The Foundation of 2 Thessalonians

Article Eight 71
  The One Sign of Jesus's Return That Everyone Needs to Know

Article Nine...79
  Was Matthew 24 Meant Solely for the Jews?

Article Ten...87
  Will the Rapture be Visible or Invisible?

Article Eleven 97
  Is Matthew 24:31 the Rapture or the Second Coming?

Article Twelve 105
  Was the Flood a Picture of the Coming of the Wrath of God?

Article Thirteen 119
  When is The Day of the Lord?

Article Fourteen 129
  Taken or Left?

Article Fifteen 137
  What is the Order of Seals, Trumpets, and Bowls?

Article Sixteen 143
  The Resurrection and Rapture Timing

Article Seventeen 155
  The Great Multitude

Article Eighteen 163
  What Direction Do the Elect Go?

Article Nineteen 169
  Is Matthew 24:31 a Gathering of Christians or Jews?

Article Twenty 179
  Is the Great Tribulation Cut Short?

Article Twenty One 185
  Only 5 Wise Virgins?

Visit Us:

The Gospel in the End Times Ministries

www.thegospelintheendtimes.com

nelson@thegospelintheendtimes.com

Our YouTube Channel

https://www.youtube.com/nelsonwalters

We have over 50 original videos on end times theology, (most under 15 minutes in length)

Article One

Will Everything Just Pan Out?

This is the second book of this type that I have published — a book derived from the transcripts of videos on my YouTube Channel. The first book, *How to Prepare for the Last Days*, began as a full-length instructional video about the last days that was itself a collection of a dozen individual videos.

This book is somewhat broader in focus and is a collection of articles that had their beginnings as transcripts in 20-plus videos about the Tribulation, the rapture, the Second Coming, the wrath of God, and just about everything else you might want to understand about what scripture has to say about these and other critical end times events. Make no mistake: If you are even a little bit concerned about your last days on earth and your eternal future, then this is a book you must read. And you must share it with those you love and with those in your church.

We begin our journey here with a rather simple question: Should you care about the end times? And related to that, you might well ask any of the following questions: Are the details really important? Do you need to change what you believe, who you listen to, or how you are preparing yourself and your families for the end? Does scripture really have all the answers? You will find your answers to all of these question in the pages of this article, and in the articles that follow.

The Second Coming of Jesus is the most universally anticipated and agreed-upon event in all of Christianity. One day, Jesus will return from heaven, resurrect the dead in Christ, reward the righteous, punish the wicked, and rule the earth as its King. As Christians this is our hope — and what we are living for.

And we are all citizens of that coming Kingdom, where Jesus the Messiah reigns as King. To make that happen, He has plans to invade this planet and overthrow the injustice and pain caused by the current earthly kingdoms; and He has given us marching orders to help prepare that overthrow. Nothing could be more important than for all of us to live our lives in the light of that future day and His instructions.

And yet, the chronology of when His glorious return will take place — before or during what many call the Tribulation — is also the most controversial issue still facing the Church.

At times, this difference of opinion has turned downright nasty. At any given moment on the internet, you can find Christians name-calling and hurling insults about this difference. How can the event the Apostle Paul termed our *blessed hope* in Titus 2:13 be the source of such unbrotherly behavior?

In order to avoid this discord, many Christians have become what can be termed *pan-rapurists*: They believe that whatever happens in the future, whatever the timing of Christ's return, *it will all pan out*. That on the issue of the return of Jesus, it doesn't matter who is right and who is wrong. They believe we need to accept and tolerate our differences on this doctrine, share the Gospel, and live out His love for others. Their position is that we can certainly do more good united than divided.

That sounds so positive doesn't it? In essentials unity, in non-essentials liberty, and in all things charity — a common doctrine among church-goers. But what if our understanding of the return of Jesus is an *essential* — a *most essential*?

The two most important days in the history of the world are the day Jesus went to the cross and the day He comes back. Is it really okay for millions to believe something false about the only one of those two days that remains? Jesus certainly didn't think so; He gave over two dozen separate instructions solely for those that enter the Tribulation period. And yet, how we prepare personally, and how we prepare our churches, depends completely on what we think will happen during that time. Will we teach Jesus's special instructions or not?

If we're among those who believe Jesus would never allow us to face the Tribulation and we're wrong — and we do enter that period *without preparing* — then we may witness — even contribute to — the starvation, death, or eternal damnation of millions. Let's not get the answer to *that* question wrong ! It will *not all just pan out* if the church enters the Tribulation.

It's likely that you already believe you have a pretty good idea what will happen during the end times. And if you're like most, you learned this view from your church or maybe in seminary. But, interestingly, in a 2016 Lifeway survey, approximately one-third of pastors believed the Church will enter the Tribulation, one-third believed they won't, and the other one-third weren't sure. On this issue, the church is divided — and confused.

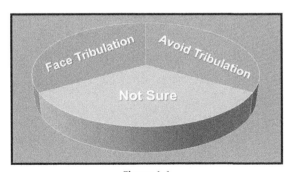

Figure 1-1

And if we turn that statistic around, two-thirds of pastors are *wrong* about this issue — whichever answer is correct!

Figure 1-2

So, can you trust what you've been taught? Or do you need to confirm it with a higher source, the *only* source that you can trust? Turns out we have *the* most important resource of all: The Holy scriptures. And Jesus is *not* confused about this issue. Not one bit! He wants us to know the truth. It's *eternally* important to Him that we know it.

We are at a cross-roads. We are asking you to stop at the intersection to consider what you believe and in which direction you would like to go. The remaining articles in this book contain a number of very fresh views on some very old and familiar scriptures — views on scriptures that I'm sure most of you have not seen before. The question for you is this: Will you honestly consider what is being presented and carefully weigh the truth of what scripture is telling you? Some of these scripture-based ideas may change your world forever. Are you willing to have the scriptures change your mind — or even change your life?

In Romans 12:2, the Apostle Paul commanded us to avoid being squeezed into the mold of the world — to avoid conforming to its pattern. He admonished us to be transformed into something new, through the renewing of our minds in God's Word.

Has your church or denomination squeezed your thinking into its pattern? Almost certainly! And on this issue, we've already seen that, from a purely statistical point of view, two-thirds of those churches and denominations are dead wrong about this issue.

Jesus expects and encourages us to change our minds about things. He expects us to renew our minds. I'm ready. Every time I open the Holy Word, I'm ready. If you're ready — really, honestly ready — to see what God has to say and to have Him change your mind on *this* issue — then you're ready to choose your path from the crossroads. Let's follow the path that leads to truth in God's Word.

Above all, let's remember what's at stake. *It's not all going to just pan out!* Remember, Jesus gave dozens of special instructions to the Apostles and to the people who will enter the Tribulation period. If it turns out that *we* are those people, we're going to need to know those instructions. Millions of souls are stake. Many within our churches, our ministries, and our own families are at risk of entering the most dangerous period in history without a playbook. Be assured: God will hold us personally responsible for making the right decisions — for ourselves and for those that we love and care about.

It's not going to be easy. It will take study, discipline, and effort to live out what Jesus has instructed us to do. This isn't something that we can train our churches to do in a week. We have to begin now. And if you're among those who believe that no preparation is necessary because you won't be around for the Tribulation, just imagine for one minute that you're wrong. If two-thirds of pastors are wrong, what makes you think your chances are any better? There won't be a *do-over*. There won't be time to prepare later.

Let me state that point again. Because it's so important. In fact, it's so important that Jesus told us a parable about it: The parable of the ten virgins. His main point in the parable was that the five foolish virgins — 50 percent! — weren't ready and didn't enter the wedding feast (heaven). The foolish virgins didn't have enough oil (the Holy Spirit) for their lamps, and the lamps went out.

Church, we need to get oil for our lamps. We need to get our churches ready. We can't be foolish virgins. We can't afford to be wrong!

Article Two

The Rapture Civil War

The church is fighting a civil war right now — a rapture civil war! Have you noticed? And it is anything but civil! In this article we're going to examine the proponents of the two main rapture theories and determine why they act the way they do. We're also going to suggest a solution to the apparent impasse which exists between the believers of the two theories.

Now, it's not difficult to find evidence of the anger and hostility which exists between those choosing up sides in the rapture game. Just look on the internet. Much of the apparent animosity exists because the leaders of the various factions are flaming the fires of discord with inflammatory rhetoric. A Pre-Wrath leader has called the Pre-Tribulation rapture theory a "satanic deception." To which the Pre-Tribulation leader suggested that the Pre-Wrath leader "used Nazi propaganda tactics." A Post-Tribulation proponent linked the unpreparedness of Pre-Tribulation followers to Pearl Harbor before the attack that led to the entry of the United States into World War II.

The inflammatory rhetoric just goes on and on. And these are the leaders of the Church! Enough already!

Sometimes the harsh words lead to real casualties. Some years ago, Marvin Rosenthal was the Director of Friends of Israel Gospel Mission. He actually lost his job because his Pre-Wrath rapture position didn't align with the beliefs favored among those sitting on the Board of Directors of the

Mission. Charles Cooper lost his position with Moody Bible Institute because of his Pre-Wrath rapture views, as well. And my personal friend, Marquis Laughlin, was taken off the air of the 200-station American Family Radio (AFR) Network because the wealthier Pre-Tribulation ministries on the network complained about Marquis and his Pre-Wrath views. They claimed that their listeners had begun asking too many questions after listening to Marquis. So to placate these wealthy, Pre-Tribulation proponents and Network donors, AFR took Marquis off the air.

And a 2017 video interview featuring Jan Markell of Olive Tree Ministries and Pastor J.D. Farag captured the two agreeing that their favored Pre-Tribulation rapture theory was being threatened by what they referred to as "satanic attacks." According to these respected Christian theologians, theories which challenged the Pre-Tribulation position were *lies*, created confusion among Christians being offered the opportunity to consider alternate theories for the first time, and were clearly *from the devil*.

I thought Bible study was from the Holy Spirit! We never hear those who favor *sprinkle* baptism calling those who prefer *immersion* baptism satanic! So why does rapture doctrine engender such deep emotion?

The reason is that the possibility of facing the Antichrist and the Great Tribulation — which includes famine, deception, martyrdom, and a falling away of the majority of church-goers — creates a worrisome scenario that has people genuinely confused, and deeply afraid. It seems that everyone who has an opinion is either trying to maintain the status quo or working desperately to change the playbook in order to improve their end times position.

In general, we could say that most of those in the Pre-Tribulation camp are perfectly happy to maintain the status quo. Given a choice, they prefer that the world stay just as it is until Jesus returns, at least as long as they can avoid pain and suffering.

Those who are Pre-Wrath and Post-Tribulation rapture supporters are at the opposite end of the spectrum. They see disaster coming like a hurricane and understand that they have an obligation to warn those in its path. Sometimes their warnings are a little too forceful — as confirmed by our ministry's own informal, man-on-the-street surveys.

Our surveys found that most Pre-Tribulation followers expressed a belief that in the end times *it will all just pan out*. Many in our survey also expressed the opinion that the scriptures are *veiled*, and it is therefore impossible to determine the truth about rapture timing. Finally, and perhaps most importantly, those surveyed felt a strong desire to avoid having their beliefs about the rapture challenged. Apparently, they simply want to believe what they believe, without having to defend those beliefs.

The results of our survey explain perfectly the comments we noted by the Pre-Tribulation leaders at the beginning of this article. It also explains why a prominent radio host would be taken off the air, just for offering arguments that allow people to re-consider their current rapture positions. And the reactions of those surveyed also explain why a noted Pre-Tribulation teacher and pastor would consider as *satanic* everything that caused their followers to doubt their position. In all of these cases, those in control clearly wanted to maintain an environment of safety in which their followers could exist without having to consider the possibility of facing the Antichrist.

But in this same survey we also learned that those favoring the Pre-Wrath and Post-Tribulation rapture theories are unwilling to grant the Pre-Tribulationists this safe place. Convinced that Christians will face the Antichrist, famine, and martyrdom, they are on a crusade to prepare as many as possible for the coming disaster. They believe that without preparation, many attending churches today — especially Pre-tribulation churches — will fall away from the faith if they face the Antichrist. They believe that preparing the believers in these churches will prevent this *apostasy*.

Unfortunately, many of these well-meaning evangelists are not particularly worried about offending others as they focus on the urgency of their crusade. And so, the rapture civil war rages on, while the unsaved watch, point fingers, and laugh at our failure to achieve consensus or practice Christian charity.

But is there a middle ground in this civil war, a place where everyone can just *get along*? There is, if we look at the problem from a hundred miles above the conflict. From that height, we can clearly see the storm coming. Removed from the proximity to our current discord, we can agree that the Tribulation is on its way. The only question we have to resolve is whether the tribulation will hit the Church.

I live in coastal North Carolina and face the possibility of hurricanes every year. Sometimes they go into the Gulf of Mexico and threaten those living in Florida, Louisiana, or

Texas. Sometimes they turn harmlessly eastward into the Atlantic Ocean. And sometimes they barrel right along the North Carolina coast — just as Hurricane Florence did in 2018. So, when a storm is forming far out in the Atlantic Ocean, we watch the forecast, sometimes for several weeks. If we are told by the forecasters that the chance of a hurricane making landfall on North Carolina is zero, we do little to prepare. Other times, when the track of the hurricane indicates that there is at least a 50% chance of the hurricane coming ashore in North Carolina, we gas up the truck and put up the hurricane shutters.

This is a perfect analogy for rapture preparation. If we can determine that the odds are 50% or greater that you, your family, and your church will face the tribulation, then you must prepare. I would say that even if the odds are only 1%, then you must prepare — because the dangers of facing the Antichrist are just too great. However, if the odds are truly zero, then there is no need to prepare.

What we need is information, so that we can — collectively — make the most informed decision possible regarding the need to prepare. Unfortunately, we cannot rely on Christian media or church leadership to help us do this. As we've already seen, most of those in a position of influence are all about maintaining a safe place where dissenting opinions and alternate interpretations are discouraged. These otherwise well-meaning Christians are fully invested in selling you on the *zero percent* forecast for the Tribulation: They want you to be so secure in your belief that you will not face the Antichrist that you will do nothing to prepare.

However, common sense should tell you that if one-in-three Christians believe otherwise, then just maybe the chance that the hurricane will strike where you live is much more likely than what you are being told. Regardless what you currently believe, you owe it to yourself to be familiar with all aspects of the rapture debate. And, ultimately, you must decide for yourself what you feel is best for yourself, your family, and your church. Do you prepare? Do you accept that there is at least some chance that you will face the Antichrist? What rapture theory you support doesn't matter near as much as what you believe about preparing for the end times.

Article Three

Will Christians Face the Great Tribulation?

In this third article, we'll examine one of the most common assertions in Christianity: That God would never allow His saints to enter the Tribulation period. How can we determine if this is true? A frequent response is that God promised us that He would keep us from the Tribulation, just as He promised that He would protect Noah from the flood. God *has* promised to protect Christians. But, did He make this *specific* promise?

I routinely hear that God would never allow Christians to suffer in the manner that would be evident if they faced the Tribulation period. But a brief walk through a cancer ward tells us that Christians suffer all the time. God clearly doesn't protect us from all suffering. While some say that God has promised to insulate Christians from *tribulation*, others say that it's His *wrath* from which God will rescue Christians. So, let's look at these two terms and see what they mean and what God's Word says about them.

The word *tribulation* is a misunderstood term. On its own it means persecution or distress. The Bible never promises that Jesus will rescue believers from tribulation. On the contrary, Jesus has actually promised us that in this world Christians *will* endure tribulation:

> *In the world you will have tribulation. But take heart; I have overcome the world.* **(John 16:33)**

In fact, Jesus takes this a step further. He tells us we are *blessed* when we are persecuted, and that suffering for His sake is a privilege:

> *Blessed are you when others revile you and persecute you.* **(Matt 5:11)**

> *For it has been granted to you that for the sake of Christ you should not only believe in him but also suffer for his sake.* **(Phil 1:2)**

Scripture contains dozens of similar passages. Jesus's best friends and most loyal followers were His disciples. Yet He allowed all but one of them to be killed in martyr's deaths. And in the recent past, faithful believers who refused to deny Jesus were horribly beheaded by ISIS. God also did not rescue them from their tribulation. So, it is wrong to say that God would never allow Christians to be persecuted or martyred. He has permitted, is still permitting, and will permit even more horrible persecution and suffering of His loyal followers. Clearly, it isn't suffering or tribulation that God has promised to keep Christians from.

Rather, it's God's *wrath*, His punishment of unbelievers, that the Bible promises Christians will be exempt from:

> *Wait for his Son from heaven, whom He raised from the dead, that is Jesus, who rescues us from the wrath to come.* **(1 Thess 1:10)**

God's wrath comes from the hand of God, and it is directed at unbelievers, not believers. An example of God's wrath is the fire that will be cast upon the earth upon Jesus's return. That clearly will be wrath; it comes from the hand of God, and it punishes *only* unbelievers.

We find, then, that God *has* promised to rescue believers before His *wrath* is poured out. He will evacuate them from the earth in an event our culture calls the rapture. The best description of this event is found in 1 Thess 4, where we observe that the Lord Jesus first descends from heaven, raises the dead, and then gathers both the dead and those still left alive into the air. But this passage doesn't mention the timing of the rapture — is it before the Tribulation, during the Tribulation, or after it?

> *For the Lord Himself will descend from heaven with a shout, with the voice of the archangel and with the trumpet of God, and the dead in Christ will rise first. Then we who are alive and remain will be caught up together with them in the clouds to meet the Lord in the air.* **(1 Thess 4:16-17)**

Those who favor a Pre-Tribulation rapture theory consider the entire Tribulation period to be God's wrath. So, they believe that the rescue will happen before the Tribulation, and they believe that God will exempt Christians from all of its events. See Figure 3-1.

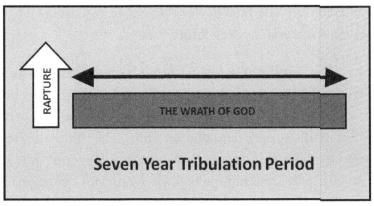

Figure 3-1

Will Christians Face the Great Tribulation?

The Pre-Wrath rapture theory assumes that the rapture happens before the wrath of God, as well. However, this theory believes that God's wrath occurs near the *end* of the Tribulation period. In this way, the church will have to endure tribulation or persecution during most of that period — and only be rescued before God pours out His wrath towards the end. This is depicted below in Figure 3-2.

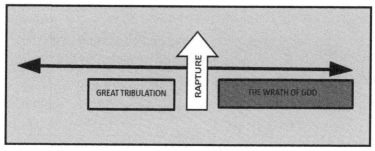

Figure 3-2

So where we read in Rev 3:10 that God will keep saints from *the hour of trial*, it is referring to keeping them from the trial of God's *wrath*:

> *I will keep you from the hour of trial that is coming on the whole world.* **(Rev 3:10)**

The two key rapture theories we have been discussing are the Pre-Tribulation theory and the Pre-Wrath theory. Both rapture theories believe that God will rescue believers from His wrath, and Rev 3:10 applies equally to both. The only difference between the theories concerns *when* that wrath begins. If we are able to biblically determine when the wrath of God begins, we can establish with reasonable certainty which of these rapture theories is the correct one — because the rapture will happen immediately before the wrath of God is poured out.

Not surprisingly, for something this critical, God has actually given us a *time marker*. In the book of Revelation, there's a clear and definitive statement of the exact day on which God's wrath begins:

> *For the great day of the wrath has come, and who is able to stand?* **(Rev 6:17)**

When we look at the context of this time marker in order to find when it takes place, we find that it occurs after a dramatic sign: The sun, and the moon, and the stars go dark, and the stars fall:

> *When he opened the sixth seal, I looked, and behold, there was a great earthquake, and the sun became black as sackcloth, the full moon became like blood, and the stars of the sky fell to the earth.* **(Rev 6:12-13)**

This same sign is recorded in numerous other books of the Bible, including Isaiah, Joel, Matthew, Mark, Luke, and Acts. Matthew's account of this sign tells us when it happens:

> *Immediately after the tribulation of those days the sun will be darkened, and the moon will not give its light, and the stars will fall from heaven.* **(Matt 24:29)**

It's clear that the sign takes place *after* the Great Tribulation. So, since the timing of the rapture is dependent on when the sign signals that God's wrath begins, and since the rapture occurs immediately before the beginning of God's wrath, the rapture must happen *after* the Great Tribulation, as well.

This is so incredibly important! Let's look at these facts again. In fact, let's build a timeline of these events:

- According to **Matt 24:29**, all of the major events take place *after* the Great Tribulation.

- At that time, the sign of the sun, moon, and stars occurs, according to both **Matt 24:29** and **Rev 6:12-14**.

- Right after that sign, the *time marker* is given in **Rev 6:17**, initiating the day of God's wrath.

- On that same day, but before His wrath is actually poured out, God rescues His saints by means of the rapture. This is found in **Matt 24:31**, where Jesus's angels gather together the elect Christians.

- Then, on that same day, after the saints are safe, the wrath of God is poured out. It begins with a fiery judgment, as seen in **Rev 8:7**.

This entire series of events is depicted in Figure 3-3.

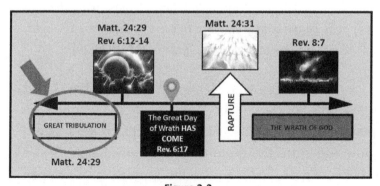

Figure 3-3

These two amazing sections of God's Word — Rev 6-8 and Matt 24 — are discussing the same events. From this, we can learn the timing of the rapture. The great *time marker*, Rev 6:17, shows us when the day of wrath begins. And the timeline which we have constructed allows us to see clearly that the wrath of God and the rapture both happen *after* the Great Tribulation. In case you haven't noticed, this timeline exactly matches the Pre-Wrath Rapture position.

Summary

Let's summarize what we've uncovered:

- First, we learned that God did not promise to keep Christians from tribulation; in fact, He promised just the opposite — that believers would experience tribulation. This means Christians are not exempt from persecution, martyrdom, and suffering — both now and in the Great Tribulation.

- Second, we learned that it's God's wrath — His punishment of unbelievers, from His own hand — from which the Bible promises Christians will be exempt. God has promised to rescue believers before His wrath is poured out, by means of the rapture.

- Third, we learned from the book of Revelation that God has given us a *time marker* that tells us exactly when the wrath of God begins. From the timeline that we created, we see that all of these events happen after the Great Tribulation:

    1. The sign in the sun, moon, and stars

    2. The time marker

3. The rapture

4. The wrath of God

- And fourth, the biblical purpose for the rapture is to protect believers from the wrath of God. Just like a SWAT team, God will send His angels to rescue the saints immediately before He pours out His wrath.

As we look back on the question we asked at the beginning of this article, we realize that Pre-Tribulation rapture proponents have been both partially right and partially wrong about God keeping Christians from the Tribulation period. He'll keep them from some of it — but not all of it. He'll protect Christians from His wrath by seeing that they are raptured before it begins. But before the rapture, these Christians will need to endure the Great Tribulation, its associated persecutions, and the potential for martyrdom.

Although this article has thus far presented a great deal of information favorable to the Pre-Wrath rapture position, not everyone finds the evidence convincing. Let's see how Pre-Tribulation rapture supporters respond to this evidence.

As we just saw in our summary, God has promised to rescue believers immediately before His wrath is poured out, and there is a specific event from the book of Revelation — what we call our *time marker* — which indicates that God's wrath begins *after* the Great Tribulation. You would think that this would resolve any debate over the timing of the rapture.

But not so fast! Those in favor of the Pre-Tribulation rapture have another point of view.

The *time marker* we uncovered occurs in Rev 6:17, in that portion of scripture in which Jesus opens a scroll with seven seals. This passage declares that the wrath of God has begun, and it occurs immediately after Jesus opens the *sixth seal* on that scroll.

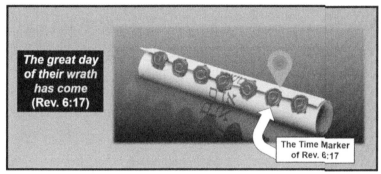

Figure 3-4

We have previously indicated that this event happens *after* the Great Tribulation; and we discussed why the rapture immediately follows this time marker verse.

Pre-Tribulation rapture followers have long proclaimed that the wrath of God actually begins *before* the *first seal*, even though this requires ignoring the clear statement of scripture that God's wrath begins *after* the *sixth seal*. So let's look at this well-known — and popular — Pre-Tribulation rapture proof.

To begin, supporters of the Pre-Tribulation rapture theory point out that it's Jesus who opens the first of the seals:

> *When the Lamb opened one of the seven seals, and I heard one of the four living creatures say with a voice like thunder, "Come!" And I looked, and behold, a white horse.* **(Rev 6:1-2)**

Will Christians Face the Great Tribulation?

After He does so, supernatural horses bring famine, war, and death to the earth. Because it's Jesus who broke the seals, Pre-Tribulation rapture supporters contend that the plagues are being caused by Him, and therefore they are His wrath.

What these well-meaning Christians miss is that Jesus isn't causing the plagues simply by opening the seals. The riders on the horses are causing the plagues. Jesus is simply *permitting* them, much as God permitted Satan to test Job. That was not God's wrath on Job, but Satan's wrath, with God's permission. There is significant evidence that this latter viewpoint is correct. Consider the following:

- The first seal is universally understood to be the coming of Antichrist, a tempter and deceiver. These traits are inconsistent with God's Holy nature; God does not cause deception, but He will allow it. So, Antichrist coming can't be part of God's doing, or of His wrath.

- Second, even more importantly, the Great Tribulation, which takes place during this period is primarily the persecution of *believers*. As we've mentioned earlier, this absolutely can't be God's wrath. God's wrath is only against *unbelievers*.

- That last point is so significant it begs repeating yet again. As we see below in 2 Thess 1:8, God's wrath is only poured out on those who don't know or love Him. Just as it wasn't God's wrath that killed those faithful believers in the Middle East, the Great Tribulation won't be His wrath either, because during that period the persecution will be primarily against believers; God won't pour out

His wrath on His own — He has *promised* us that He will not do that.

> *Inflicting vengeance on those who do not know God and on those who do not obey the gospel of our Lord Jesus.* **(2 Thess 1:8)**

The Great Tribulation will be just exactly what Jesus termed it: tribulation, *not* wrath. Tribulation is something that Jesus has told us we will face in this life. This is a critical point that nearly all Pre-Tribulation supporters miss or choose to ignore.

These reasons alone should be sufficient to convince you that the Pre-Tribulation rapture position isn't biblically accurate. But God was so concerned that we get this point right, that we know beyond a shadow of a doubt when His wrath begins, that He placed a legal proceeding — complete with witnesses — in the text of Rev 6. So, let's call the first witnesses.

When Jesus opens the fifth seal, the souls of martyrs from all the ages will cry out for God's justice to come, and for Him to end the Great Tribulation. Notice the words of their testimony: They say that, as of the fifth seal, God has *not yet* begun to judge and not yet begun to avenge.

> *They cried out with a loud voice, "O Sovereign Lord, holy and true, how long before you will judge and avenge our blood on those who dwell on the earth?"* **(Rev 6:10)**

There is no way a righteous God would pour out His wrath before judging! Plus, at that point, God hasn't taken action to avenge, either. This is amazingly clear evidence that the wrath of God will not have taken place before the fifth seal. Logically, if it didn't start by the fifth seal, it couldn't have started with the first seal or before the Tribulation, either. This is critically important.

What we have been calling the time marker verse of Rev 6:17 is eyewitness testimony, as well:

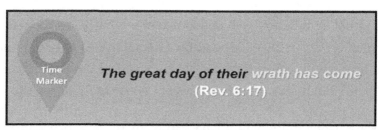

Figure 3-5

When unbelievers look up into the sky after the sixth seal and see Jesus on His Throne, they will know that the time has come for His wrath. Then they will cry out to the rocks of the earth to hide them from Jesus's presence.

Now, we know that legal matters are determined by two witnesses — this was especially true during biblical times. We now have our two sets of witnesses:

- *At the fifth seal*, the martyrs testify that the wrath had not yet begun.

- *After the sixth seal*, the witnesses testify that the wrath of God finally has come, or begun.

Both of these eyewitness testimonies absolutely preclude the wrath of God beginning before the Tribulation period or at the first seal. Scripture presents a legally binding argument that the wrath of God, the justification for the rapture, happens *after* the sixth seal, which occurs *after* the Great Tribulation.

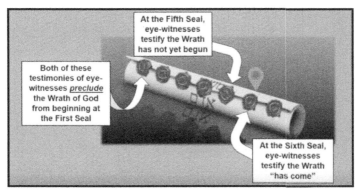

Figure 3-6

As you've probably grasped by now, the time marker verse of Rev 6:17 might be one of the most important verses in the rapture debate. For that reason, the verb translated *has come* in the verse has been questioned. This Greek verb is found in the *aorist* tense, a tense not found in the English language. According to Dr. David Mathewson of Denver Seminary, aorist tense can assume past tense, present tense, or even future tense, depending on the context of the word. Some Pre-Tribulationists have therefore said, "Well, then, perhaps *has come* in the time marker verse is actually in the past tense. Perhaps it should be h*ad come,* and the reference should be all the way back to the beginning of the Tribulation. Perhaps it's saying God's wrath *had come* way back at that point!"

Well, that *would* be something. If it were true. But remember, Dr. Mathewson said *context determines the tense.* And what was that context? As we have just discussed, right before the time marker verse, all of the un-righteous see Jesus on His Throne in the sky and beg the rocks to hide them from Jesus's face and from His wrath.

> *Then…everyone, slave and free, hid themselves in the caves and among the rocks of the mountains, calling to the mountains and rocks, "Fall on us and hide us from the face of him who is seated on the throne, and from the wrath."* **(Rev 6:15-16)**

This is a *present tense* reality to them. No one asks to be hidden from something that happened years earlier. That would be complete nonsense. The only possible timing for this verse is present tense — *has come*. That is why every major English translation of the Bible translates this verse as *has come* — including the King James, the New King James, the ESV, the NIV, and the NASB. There is no wiggle room on this point.

So, hopefully, what we have resolved is that the timing of God's wrath — appearing as it does *after the sixth seal* — is consistent with the Pre-Wrath rapture. But because this theory is not well understood, let's take a few moments to visualize what this theory looks like:

- The seven-year tribulation begins with a three-and-a-half-year period Jesus calls the *beginning of the birth pangs*. This period is marked by the emergence of false Christs, war, famine, and earthquakes.

- At the midpoint of the seven-year tribulation, the Antichrist is revealed.

- After the revealing of Antichrist, the Great Tribulation begins. This will be a time of unprecedented persecution of believers and evangelical testimony to the unbelieving.

- The Great Tribulation does not last the entire final half of the Tribulation period; it is cut short for the sake of the elect, as we are told in **Matt 24:22**: It is the sign of the sun, moon, and stars that cuts it short.

- It is at this moment that Jesus appears in the sky, and His angels rapture believers, as reported **Matt 24:31**. This happens in the second half of the Tribulation period; and believers spend the remaining time in heaven, safe from the wrath of God, which will be poured out on the earth.

- God pours out His wrath on unbelievers in the form of the seven trumpet and seven bowl judgments.

- Finally, after the wrath of God is poured out, Jesus and the saints return to the earth — in an event we know as the Second Coming — to fight the battle of Armageddon.

The timeline of the Tribulation period from a Pre-Wrath perspective appears as depicted in Figure 3-7.

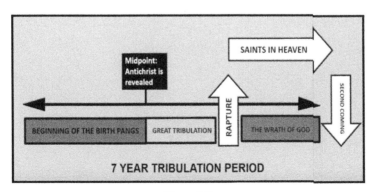

Figure 3-7

The Pre-Wrath rapture theory is an improved version of the Pre-Tribulation or Post-Tribulation rapture theories, simply because it is consistent with all of scripture and eliminates the inconsistencies that plague each of these older theories.

In the next article we will answer the question that is probably on your mind right now: "Why would God permit such suffering as will occur during the Great Tribulation, rather than rescuing believers first?"

Article Four

Why Does God Permit Great Tribulation?

In the previous article we clearly demonstrated from scripture that God will not rescue Christians from persecution and martyrdom. Rather, God will rescue Christians from His *wrath*. And, and as we've seen, that wrath happens after the Great Tribulation. This realization is unsettling — even frightening — to many.

But there are still Pre-Tribulation Rapture scholars who will argue that there is no need for Christians to enter the Great Tribulation. They will argue that God's purpose during the Great Tribulation is to make a final attempt to bring unsaved Jews and non-Jews to a saving knowledge of Jesus. These scholars point out that Christians are already saved, so they don't require this final effort to save them. And they therefore argue that God can simply remove them from this difficult time and use some other means to bring salvation to the Jews.

But this argument misses a major part of God's purpose for this time period — which is to *bless* Christians who enter the Tribulation:

> *Blessed are those who have been persecuted for the sake of righteousness, for theirs is the kingdom of heaven.*
> **(Matt 5:10)**

Now, you may find yourself wondering whether the Great Tribulation could be considered a blessing. Yes, Jesus told us directly that persecution *is* a blessing; it may not be what we would choose for ourselves, but a Holy God knows best.

Why Does God Permit Great Tribulation?

Nearly all scholars agree that one of God's purposes for the Great Tribulation is the salvation of unsaved Jews and Gentiles. The scriptures confirm this. The concept of testimony is found three times in the end times teachings of Jesus in Matthew, Mark, and Luke; and it's found nine times in Revelation. But, who better to provide that testimony than those who already know the New Testament and the voice of the Holy Spirit? Who better than those who are already believers?

But why do this during the Tribulation, when even speaking the name of Jesus will be a capital crime? Because, as Luke tells us, it will offer the greatest opportunity to bear witness:

> *But before all his they will lay their hands on you and persecute you ... This will be your opportunity to bear witness.* **(Luke 21:12-13)**

When those who are unsaved see thousands of Christians risking their lives to witness and offer testimony to them, they will be deeply moved, creating opportunities for millions of souls to be saved. The unsaved may not be paying attention to Christians now, but they will be then.

We see, then, that the *first blessing* is that Christians who enter the Tribulation will have the greatest opportunity the world has ever known to evangelize to the lost and bring glory to God. They will shine like lights in the world:

> *That you may be blameless and innocent, children of God without blemish in the midst of a crooked and twisted generation, among whom you shine as lights in the world.* **(Phil 2:15)**

This is why believers were created and saved: To witness and save others — not to live comfortable lives and then be whisked away at the very moment of the world's greatest need.

When persecution and tribulation arose in the book of Acts, believers scattered to other regions in an effort to escape. In the process, their testimony increased, and more souls were saved:

> *And there arose on the day a great persecution against the church in Jerusalem, and they were all scattered throughout the regions of Judea and Samaria…those who were scattered went about preaching the word.* **(Acts 8:1, 4)**

It was precisely *because of* persecution that the Gospel was able to spread. During the Great Tribulation, it will be exactly the same.

Consider the current state of Christianity in the world today. On one hand, we have Christians who faithfully serve the Lord in ministry to both the saved and unsaved. On the other hand, we have church-goers who allow politics, prosperity, and self-focus to distort the meaning of God's Gospel. Might it be the Great Tribulation that causes the second group to realize how wrongly they have viewed God's will? Perhaps that is part of God's purpose for the Great Tribulation.

In the end times we will realize that the focus our churches have placed on buildings, music programs, and other amenities have been misplaced. What we should have been doing all along is preparing the world by taking the Gospel to all the nations. The Church in the Tribulation will be much more like the Church of Acts.

Why Does God Permit Great Tribulation?

In the Tribulation Church, there will be saints who emulate Stephen, Silas, Philip, Paul, and Barnabas. Jesus will sing of their exploits and love them forever in the Kingdom. They will live as if this world is not their home, because it isn't. Their true home is in the Kingdom of God. And yes, these saints will also be empowered by the Holy Spirit in miraculous ways we don't routinely see now.

So, honestly consider your current life. Do you prefer it as it is, or would you rather be one of the saints of the Most High, living out the Church of Acts that is to come? During the Tribulation, the *true* Church will reach its zenith and return to a Church of Acts environment, in which believers will worship in spirit and truth. This will be the *second blessing*:

> *The true worshipers will worship the Father in spirit and truth, for the Father is seeking such people to worship him.* **(John 4:23)**

And, shockingly, a *third blessing* is that in the Tribulation God will permit saints to help in overcoming Satan. The weapons of their warfare will be the blood of the Lamb, their testimony, and the very fact that they did not love their lives more than they loved the Lord Himself:

> *And they have conquered him by the blood of the Lamb and by the word of their testimony, for they loved not their lives even unto death.* **(Rev 12:11)**

In stark contrast to the Tribulation Church of heroes and saints, the Pre-Tribulation rapture theory presumes that all Christians are raptured *before* the trials and the testimony. In this scenario, the task of testifying to the unsaved is left to 144,000 Jews, who are currently unsaved themselves. This makes absolutely no sense! These Jews have no knowledge of the New Testament. And besides, there are several scriptural reasons why they will *not* be evangelists:

1. Most importantly, nowhere in scripture are the 144,000 called evangelists, nor does the Bible *ever* show them evangelizing anyone.

2. They aren't saved until *after* the sixth seal is opened. As we have learned, this is *after* the Great Tribulation and right before the wrath of God is poured out. This means they will *still be unsaved* during the entire Great Tribulation, when evangelism would be needed the most! This is yet another critical point that Pre-Tribulation rapture followers miss or choose to neglect.

3. Finally, it will be impossible for the 144,000 to evangelize, because they are going to be *in heaven*, not on earth. This is a very poorly understood concept. Rev 14:2-4 makes it clear that not only are the 144,000 in heaven, but they are standing before the Throne, singing a song only they know. They are *firstfruits*, the very first to be raptured to heaven. Again, a mistaken view of rapture timing obscures the understanding of most scholars regarding the role of the 144,000:

   I heard a voice from heaven ... and they were singing a new song before the throne and before the four living creatures and before the elders. No one could learn that song except the 144,000 who had been redeemed from the earth ... These have been redeemed from mankind as first-fruits for God and the Lamb. **(Rev 14:2-4)**

Why Does God Permit Great Tribulation?

Finally, as a *fourth blessing*, God will be ever-present with the saints during the Tribulation. Do you remember how you felt God's presence during and following the 9/11 attacks? How much greater will be His presence during the Great Tribulation?

> *God is our refuge and strength, a very present help in trouble.* **(Psm 46:1)**

The saints who endure and overcome that period will experience God in ways few of us have or ever will. Do we honestly believe that our currently comfortable lives are really better than they would be if we could rely on God's constant presence?

So, for all of these reasons, the 144,000 aren't evangelists — which only makes sense. That's a job for the Church.

Will you join the unfinished story during the Tribulation and become part of the coming Church of Acts? Will you be part of the group of blessed saints Jesus sings about for eternity? This is perhaps the most important question you have yet to answer in your lifetime. Please don't let a mistaken view of God's role for the Tribulation prevent you from overcoming.

In the next article, we will find confirmations in the writings of the Apostle Paul for everything we've learned about thus far. We will also find reasons why it is important for us to examine the scriptures ourselves and to avoid relying completely on the teachings of others.

Article Five

Is Rapture the Best Word to Use?

Throughout this book so far, we have established clearly that scriptures support a Pre-Wrath rapture and that many of the Pre-Tribulation axioms simply aren't biblical. Even so, I'm sure you still have questions. In this and subsequent articles we will continue to examine the issues and provide you with answers. In this article, we will look at the word our culture uses to describe the transportation of believers into the presence of Jesus.

The word *rapture* isn't found in the Bible. That's because it's an English word. It's derived from the Latin *rapio*, and *rapio* was a translation of the original Greek word *harpazo*, which is found in the most descriptive rapture passage in the Bible:

> *For the Lord Himself will descend from heaven with a shout, with the voice of the archangel and with the trumpet of God, and the dead in Christ will rise first. Then we who are alive and remain will be caught up together with them in the clouds to meet the Lord in the air, and so we shall always be with the Lord.* **(1 Thess 4:16-17)**

So the word rapture is a Bible-based *idea*, and it's an acceptable word to use. But is it the *best* choice of words?

Although there were *harpazo's* in ancient times, it is only used once in end times context throughout the entire New Testament. So although rapture is a legitimate choice of words, the term *gather together* might be a better choice. The term is used 11 times in the New Testament to describe the future transportation of believers into the presence of Jesus, and it was the only term Jesus used to describe this event. So we need to ask ourselves why the term rapture in so much in vogue, when the term *gather together* was clearly preferred by New Testament persona, including Jesus, John the Baptist, and Paul.

The term *gather together* was actually the primary term used by the early church; and its use helped then, as it does now, to establish the actual order of events in the end times. In other words, it helps to prove rapture timing. So was there something more contrived afoot in the use of the term *rapture*? Perhaps. And we'll explore that some more in this article.

The first use of *gather together* as a term for the rescue of the saints was by John the Baptist, before Jesus's ministry even began. It is mentioned in Matt 3:12, where the description of the gathering of wheat into the barn is a picture of the rapture, wherein the wheat is symbolic of believers, and the barn represents heaven:

> *His winnowing fork is in His hand, and He will thoroughly clear His threshing floor; and He will gather His wheat into the barn, but He will burn up the chaff with unquenchable fire.* **(Matt 3:12)**

Jesus expanded on this illustration in the parable of the wheat and the tares in Matt 13:30. Again, wheat represents believers, and they are gathered into the barn of heaven at the same time unbelievers are burned with fire:

> *Allow both to grow together until the harvest; and in the time of the harvest I will say to the reapers, "First gather up the tares and bind them in bundles to burn them up; but gather the wheat into my barn."* **(Matt 13:30)**

Greek is an expressive language, with many words to describe the action of gathering. Both John and Jesus used the word *sunago*, which is an assisted type of gathering. In the parable of the wheat and the tares, Jesus explained that the gathering will be done by angels. They are the gatherers, those doing the assisting.

But how do these early teachings demonstrate rapture timing? In the scripture references above, we see that a division of the righteous and the un-righteous occurs upon the return of Jesus. The righteous are gathered to be raptured (into the barn) and the un-righteous are gathered to be burned with fire. Notice that it is a burning of the wicked (weeds) in fiery judgment, not simply their entering into the Tribulation period. The rapture happens on the *same day* as the fiery judgment. So that clearly cannot be a Pre-Tribulation event.

In fact, Jesus specifically *prohibits* an early gathering. In Matt 13:30 He taught that both the wheat and the weeds should grow together until the harvest. By this Jesus specifies that *both* the believers and the wicked will exist together until the time of the harvest, at which time the believers will be ushered into the presence of the Lord and the wicked will be burned with fire. That is *not* the picture of a Pre-Tribulation rapture. In fact, it *precludes* it!

And this wasn't the only time that Jesus taught about a same-day rescue of believers and a burning of unbelievers. Jesus repeatedly taught this doctrine. For example, Jesus equated the days of Lot with His return:

> *But on the day that Lot went out from Sodom it rained fire and brimstone from heaven and destroyed them all.*

Is Rapture the Best Word to Use?

> *It will be just the same on the day that the Son of Man is revealed.* **(Luke 17:29-30)**

In scripture, Lot represents all believers, and he is saved by angels on the same day fire rains down and burns the wicked in Sodom. Jesus also compared his coming to the flood of Noah:

> *And just as it happened in the days of Noah, so it will be also in the days of the Son of Man: they were eating, they were drinking, they were marrying, they were being given in marriage, until the day that Noah entered the ark, and the flood came and destroyed them all.* **(Luke 17:26-27)**

Remember that in Luke we read that the wicked lived normal lives until the day when Noah entered the ark and the flood came. In this example, Noah represents the righteous believers, and he is lifted above the wrath of God, while the un-righteous are destroyed. All on the exact same day.

Now, we know that Noah began loading animals seven days prior to the flood. We see this in Gen 7. But in Luke 17 and Gen 7:13, it is clear that Noah and his family entered the ark *on the same exact day* as the flood began:

> *On the very same day Noah and Shem and Ham and Japheth, the sons of Noah, and Noah's wife and the three wives of his sons with them, entered the ark.* **(Gen 7:13)**

And in his New Testament letters, Paul elaborated on this same day rapture and fiery judgment:

> *For after all it is only just for God to repay with affliction those who afflict you, and to give relief to you who are afflicted and to us as well when the Lord Jesus*

> *will be revealed from heaven with His mighty angels in flaming fire, dealing out retribution to those who do not know God and to those who do not obey the gospel of our Lord Jesus.* **(2 Thess 1:6-8)**

Paul said that the wrath of God will be poured out on those who persecute the Church at the same time that Jesus provides relief to believers in the form of a rapture. All of this happens when Jesus appears to the whole world in flaming fire.

Both Jesus and Paul explicitly taught a separation of the righteous and the un-righteous on the Day of the Lord, toward the end of the Tribulation. So where is the Pre-Tribulation rapture? The answer is, quite simply, *nowhere*! Not only is the Pre-tribulation rapture *not* shown in scripture, it isn't even implied!

But, if we look for a rapture that uses the term *gathered together*, we find it instantly. The rapture has been there all the time in the passages of Matt, Mark, and Luke. We just had to look for the term *gather together* to find it.

And look at this much-overlooked passage. Look at how specific it is:

> *Then they will see the son of man coming on the clouds with great power and glory. And then He will send forth the angels and will gather together His elect from the four winds, from the farthest end of the earth to the farthest end of heaven.* **(Mark 13:26-27)**

The gathering of believers is *from the earth to the farthest end of heaven*. Is there any mistaking that this is the rapture, by whatever term we choose to call it?

In contrast, let's look at a traditional Pre-Tribulation rapture proof that considers the separation of the righteous and the unrighteous. The word *church* is not found in the *bulk* of the book of Revelation, Chapters 4 through 21:

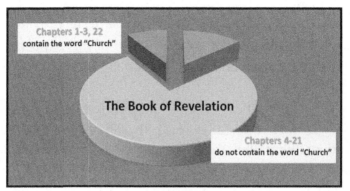

Figure 5-1

Historically, Pre-Tribulation proponents have argued that the word *Church* was missing because they held that all believers (the Church) were raptured into heaven before the Tribulation Period even began. But this argument was long ago disproven, and it is not much used as a proof by academics anymore. Let's see why.

Although the argument sounds good, careful examination makes clear that the word *church* as it's used in Revelation never refers to the Church Universal or to all believers. Instead, it refers only to the specific *seven churches* to which Jesus sends letters. So the word *church* is used as a proper name in Revelation — for example, the Church of Ephesus. It can also be used to refer to all seven churches as a group. And since the letters to those seven churches all appear within the first 3 chapters of Revelation (or at the end), that's where the word church is found, as well. The absence of the word *church* elsewhere in Revelation has absolutely nothing to do with a rapture.

Christians are frequently mentioned in Revelation using the terms *bondservants* and *saints*. Why does John not use the term *church* to refer to Christians? Perhaps it's because not everyone who attends church is a Christian. Maybe John chooses not to confuse believers with church-goers. True believers will all make it into heaven. The same cannot be said of all church-goers.

In conclusion, what can we say about the use of these terms *rapture* and *gather together*? Just that in the 1800's a conscious effort was made to move away from using the term gather together and instead make use of the term rapture. Was that a conscious decision, designed to deflect our attention away from the proper sequence of end times events, thereby facilitating the feel-good Pre-Tribulation rapture scenario? Perhaps.

Let's let the Apostle Paul have the last word on this discussion with regard to the coming of our Lord Jesus Christ and our gathering together with Him:

> *Now we request you, brethren, with regard to the coming of our Lord Jesus Christ and our gathering together to Him ... Let no one in any way deceive you, for it will not come unless the apostasy comes first, and the man of lawlessness is revealed, the son of destruction.* **(2 Thess 2:1, 3)**

Article Six

Let No One Deceive You

Before we begin this article, let me remind you that the things you are learning in these pages have eternal consequences. You are to be congratulated for your dedication in coming this far. But there is so much more to be learned.

Though challenging, I encourage you to be like the Bereans from the book of Acts in the New Testament. Faithfully examine all that you read here; then determine for yourself whether what we have presented is true, based on your own study of the scriptures:

> *They received the word with all eagerness, examining the scriptures daily to see if these things were so.* **(Acts 17:12)**

In this article, we will see an example in which poor scholarship resulted in the advancement of an erroneous truth to several generations of Christians — all because the Christians hadn't checked things out properly for themselves.

This modern incident of poor scholarship involves Paul's 2nd letter to the Thessalonians. At the time, the Thessalonians were undergoing severe persecution; and because of this, rumors began to circulate among them that perhaps they were living during the wrath of God. Consequently, they began to feel that they may have missed the rescue that is the *rapture*.

So, Paul sent them his 2nd letter to assure them that the rapture he told them about in his 1st letter hadn't happened and to clarify for them the order of end times events. In Chapter 2 of his epistle, Paul focuses on the Thessalonian's concern that the return of Jesus and the rapture had passed them by.

First, he mentions the coming of Jesus, which Paul then links to the *gathering together*. Notice that it is the gathering of the *faithful* to Jesus, not the gathering of unsaved Jews or other groups. This is the rapture which Jesus depicts in the following passage:

> *And He will send forth His angels with a great trumpet and they will gather together His elect from the four winds, from one end of the sky to the other.* **(Matt 24:31)**

Paul then gets to his main point — that the Thessalonians aren't to be alarmed that they had missed the rapture or that they were now living during the Day of the Lord, which is the wrath of God, and which immediately follows the rapture:

> *Now concerning the coming of our Lord Jesus Christ and our being gathered together to him, we ask you, brothers, not to be quickly shaken in mind or alarmed, either by a spirit or a spoken word, or a letter seeming to be from us, to the effect that the day of the Lord has come.* **(2 Thess 2:1-2)**

Paul then shows them why they weren't to be concerned. He tells them two things have to happen before the rapture can take place. These will be the signs that will inform Christians that the rapture is coming. And if they are signs, then they have to be recognizable by Christians in any generation:

> *Let no one deceive you in any way. For that day will not come, unless the rebellion comes first, and the man of lawlessness is revealed, the son of destruction, who*

> *opposes and exalts himself against every so-called God or object of worship, so that he takes his seat in the temple of God, proclaiming himself to be God.* **(2 Thess 2:3-4)**

The *first sign* will be a *rebellion* from the faith, what many translations term *apostasy*. We are experiencing a minor falling away today in many of our own churches. But how much apostasy is needed to achieve the *falling away?* Only the apostasy during the Great Tribulation, the one Jesus references in Matt 24:10, can possibly qualify as a recognizable falling away. And this is an event during the Tribulation period:

> *At that time many will fall away and will betray one another and hate one another.* **(Matt 24:10)**

The *second sign* will be the revealing of the Antichrist at the midpoint of the Tribulation period. Now some believe this *revealing* will happen at the beginning of the Tribulation, when some expect the Antichrist to sign a peace treaty. But Paul is clear that the *revealing* will occur when the Antichrist sits in the new Temple of God and shows himself as if he is God — the *abomination of desolation*. This is a recognizable, one-of-a-kind event that can therefore be considered a sign. Daniel is also quite clear that the coming of Antichrist will be the abomination of desolation at the midpoint of the Tribulation period:

> *For half of the week he shall put an end to sacrifice and offering. and on the wing of abominations shall come one who makes desolate.* **(Dan 9:27)**

The Antichrist may or may not sign a treaty, but either way it won't be a recognizable sign, since treaties are signed every day. No one will really know who the Antichrist is with certainty until he is revealed by sitting in the Temple of God at the abomination. So, we have two firm events that must happen prior to the rapture.

Let's look at this graphically. The rapture must come *after* the revealing of Antichrist at the midpoint, and *after* the Great Tribulation. Because both of these events are during the Tribulation, the rapture can't come *before* the Tribulation. Therefore, by definition, it can't be a Pre-Tribulation rapture. Rather, it must be a Pre-Wrath rapture.

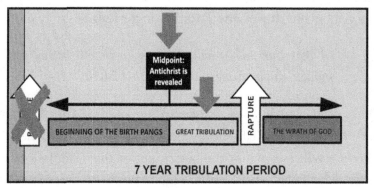

Figure 6-1

Only a Pre-Wrath rapture meets all of the requirements set forth by Paul. Because the rapture must take place *after* the revealing of Antichrist at the midpoint, the Pre-Tribulation rapture is eliminated as a possibility. Because the rapture must take place *after* the Great Tribulation, the Mid-Tribulation rapture theory is eliminated.

And remember that the Thessalonians were worried that they were living during the wrath of God and had missed the rapture? Well, if they had been taught by Paul to believe in a Post-Tribulation rapture, they wouldn't have been complaining at all. Because the Post-Tribulation theory holds that believers will live through the wrath of God before being raptured — the

Thessalonians would have expected to be severely persecuted by God! The Post-Tribulation rapture theory can therefore be eliminated, as well.

Only the Pre-Wrath rapture uniquely places the rapture before the wrath of God and after the Great Tribulation and the revealing of Antichrist.

When Pre-Tribulation rapture followers are confronted with scripture passages that challenge their position, they often attempt to manipulate the meaning of underlying Greek words. In this case the word is *apostasia*, which has been properly translated *rebellion,* and is also correctly translated as *falling away*. However, in E. Schuyler English's 1954 book, *Rethinking The Rapture,* he proposed that it can mean departure. In his mind, it was a code word for the rapture of the church.

In this way, English suggested that what Paul really meant to say was that the rapture comes first, then the revealing of Antichrist, and then the wrath of God. So, however wrong it was, the Pre-Tribulation rapture theory used this mistranslation to gain a foothold in eschatological communities. And for over 60 years this theory has circulated in Pre-Tribulational circles.

But let's look at this word as a good Berean. *Apostasia* is used five times in the Greek Old Testament and twice in the New Testament — and it *always* means *rebellion from the faith.* Scripture interprets scripture. This word *never* means departure or rapture in the Bible. Not only does it not mean departure in the Bible, but Dr. Paul Feinberg has analyzed Greek literature in the 300-year period surrounding the writing of 2 Thess; and in the 355 uses of this word during that period, it *never* means departure — not even once! And what makes this even more impressive is that Dr. Feinberg, at least currently, is a Pre-

Tribulationist. That is why every major translation of the Bible translates *apostasia* as rebellion, and *never* as rapture or departure.

And yet, despite that overwhelming evidence, a literal Who's Who of Pre-Tribulation scholars have at one time or another accepted English's original mis-translation. Like links in a chain, these men have cited the work of their predecessors on this subject — one man's error propagated through the Church for over 60 years. You may be familiar with some of these names:

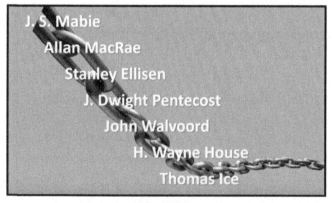

Figure 6-2

And perhaps that is why Paul was so emphatic that we not allow anyone to deceive us in any way about this truth — even if it comes from renowned teachers with advanced degrees, is spoken by the heads of denominations, or is preached from the pulpit by your own pastor. Paul says that we must not let them deceive us about *this truth*, which is that the rapture comes after the Great Tribulation and the revealing of Antichrist:

> *Let no one deceive you in any way. For that day will not come, unless the rebellion comes first, and the man of lawlessness is revealed* **(2 Thess 2:3)**

So in all things regarding the scriptures, you must be a good Berean; you must always weigh the valuable teaching of others against your own understanding of scripture:

> *Now these were more noble-minded than those in Thessalonica, for they received the word with great eagerness, examining the scriptures daily to see whether these things were so.* **(Acts 17:11)**

And Paul shows us why — in frightening fashion. Look at his stern warning about knowing this truth: That the Antichrist will come with power, displaying false signs and wonders:

> *The coming of the lawless one is by the activity of Satan with all power and false signs and wonders* **(2 Thess 2:9-10)**

In Matt 24:24 Jesus said that this man would even deceive the elect, if that were possible. And those he will deceive are the ones who refuse to love the truth or believe the truth. What truth is that? Jesus is the truth — the way, the truth, and the life. So ultimately it is believing in and loving Jesus:

> *Because they refused to love the truth and so be saved. Therefore God sends them a strong delusion, so that they may believe what is false, in order that all may be condemned who did not believe the truth* **(2 Thess 2:10-12)**

But the truth that Paul mentions in this passage is related to the coming of Antichrist, the great deceiver. So Paul is saying that the ones who will fall away in that rebellion are those who will believe Antichrist's false signs and worship him and not Jesus. Think about it, these may be your friends and neighbors. They may be members of the very church you worship at on Sunday morning.

And why will they worship the Antichrist? Well, for many reasons. But perhaps the main reason may be that they don't expect that they will face him. Not realizing that Christians will face the Antichrist is perhaps the *greatest risk* of believing the Pre-Tribulation rapture theory. So, when unsaved church-goers do see the Antichrist in the new Temple of God, they might say, "This can't be the Antichrist, because we have been taught that we are to be raptured first."

Imagine the danger of not knowing it is the Antichrist, when this man offers his saving grace in the form of his mark. Will the unsaved in our pews accept it and the eternal damnation that goes with it — because in their minds this can't be the Antichrist, and that can't be his mark? Or imagine the anger and distrust other unsaved church-goers will feel toward their pastors for having failed to warn them that they would face the Antichrist. Will millions walk away from the faith saying, "If church leaders were wrong about something this important, might they also have been wrong about Jesus being the Messiah?" So you see: There is indeed great risk for those who believe the Pre-Tribulation rapture theory.

Earlier, we learned in the parable of the ten virgins that Jesus told us that *half* of those who are waiting for His return will *not* be raptured into heaven — they aren't saved. And Paul let us know that many of those who are unprepared to face Antichrist will be deceived and fall away. Might these be the same 50% Jesus warned us about?

But instead, what if your church taught the truth that Paul presents — that Christians will face the Antichrist — rather than falsely assuring them that they will not have to face persecution or deception. Might the Holy Spirit move in that moment to save many who right now are just pseudo-Christians, those who want His blessings, but don't really love Jesus enough to die for Him? That is a question that every one of us needs to answer.

I bet it has come as a surprise that teaching proper rapture timing can be an evangelistic outreach opportunity to the unsaved within your own church!

Article Seven

The Foundation of 2 Thessalonians

As we have learned, the Thessalonians at the time of Paul were concerned because they thought that they were living during God's wrath and had missed the rapture. Paul wrote his second letter to them to reassure them that they hadn't missed the rapture. He stressed that they could know this for certain because two signs had to take place before the rapture and the Day of the Lord. And because those signs will happen during the Tribulation period, they preclude a Pre-Tribulation rapture.

We have also discussed arguments that Pre-Tribulation proponents have used to combat these scriptural truths, based in part on the translation of a single Greek word *apostasy*. And we have seen that generations of Pre-Tribulation scholars have supported a mis-translation of that word. This is what is known as a *micro-proof* — a selective focusing on a single word or idea to support a position.

Although we have thoroughly refuted the Pre-Tribulation arguments, we will offer in this article yet another proof that demonstrates how 2 Thess disproves the Pre-Tribulation rapture theory. And it's a *macro* proof, a big-picture proof.

When Paul wrote this epistle, it contained a number of concepts that Paul hadn't written about before. Where did he get these ideas? Certainly, from the Holy Spirit. But did he base this teaching on a previous scriptural passage, as well? If so, what was that previous scripture?

The Foundation of 2 Thessalonians

In this article we will show that it was Matt 24, the Olivet Discourse. This is *a new and revolutionary discovery.* It demonstrates that Paul was paraphrasing and explaining the concepts in Matt 24, concepts that negate a Pre-Tribulation rapture.

Of course, we previously provided a similar discussion on how 1 Thess. 4-5 is based on Matt 24, as well. Matthew 24 seems to have been Paul's primary endtimes reference text. However, this article concentrates on 2 Thess And remember that although today's Bibles divide 2 Thess into chapters and verses, the original epistle was a letter meant to be read aloud in a single hearing. It was a unified whole.

Paul begins this letter by explaining to the Thessalonians that what they are experiencing is *tribulation not wrath*:

> *Therefore, we ourselves speak proudly of you among the churches of God for your perseverance and faith in the midst of all your persecutions and afflictions which you endure.* **(2 Thess 1:4)**

In an earlier article we explained how tribulation is something all Christians are promised to experience.

Paul continues by explaining that this tribulation is a sign to them that they are worthy of the coming Kingdom and that it is not something that is happening to them as punishment:

> *This is a plain indication of God's righteous judgment so that you will be considered worthy of the kingdom of God, for which indeed you are suffering.* **(2 Thess 1:5)**

The coming Great Tribulation will be just such a sign to Christians, and enduring it will be a sign of worthiness, not punishment.

After making that clear, Paul begins to show the Thessalonians why true believers can't be living during the wrath of God:

> *For after all it is only just for God to repay with affliction those who afflict you, and to give relief to you who are afflicted and to us as well when the Lord Jesus will be revealed from heaven.* **(2 Thess 1:6-7)**

Paul explains that God will afflict the un-repentant on the same day that He gives relief in the form of the rapture to the righteous. What day is that? It will be the day that Jesus is revealed from heaven. It is a same-day wrath and rapture. And this will not be a silent or secret revealing:

> *And to give relief to you who are afflicted and to us as well when the Lord Jesus will be revealed from heaven with His mighty angels in flaming fire.* **(2 Thess 1:7)**

Jesus will be revealed with his angels and in flaming fire for the whole world to see. What is this flaming fire? Why the *Shekinah Glory* of the Lord!

At this point, Paul makes an interesting remark about this day, which absolutely time marks it as the day of the rapture. He tells us that he and the rest of his mission team will be given relief on this same exact day. Now, clearly Paul and his fellow missionaries are dead. They can only receive relief at the resurrection of the righteous, which must occur on the same day as the rapture.

The Foundation of 2 Thessalonians

And look what Paul says happens to the un-righteous on this same day:

> *These will pay the penalty of eternal destruction, away from the presence of the Lord and from the glory of His power, when He comes to be glorified in His saints on that day, and to be marveled at among all who have believed — for our testimony to you was believed.* **(2 Thess 1:9-10)**

They face eternal destruction. Is that what we think happens at a Pre-Tribulation rapture? Certainly not! Every Pre-Tribulation supporter believes that millions — even hundreds of millions — come to faith during the Tribulation. This passage in 2 Thess completely disproves the Pre-Tribulation rapture position, because Paul clearly says that the un-righteous face eternal destruction on that day. And where did Paul derive this teaching from? From Matt 24.

Let's look more closely at where he found all these concepts. In just a short passage from Chapter 1 of 2 Thess there are six comparisons with Matt 24:

1. Both Matt 24 and 2 Thess use the term *that day* or *the day*. 2 Thess references the days of Noah, and both refer to a same day wrath and rapture.

2. Both passages refer to the revealing or appearing of Jesus.

3. In both passages, Jesus comes from heaven with His angels.

4. In both passages, He comes in His great *Shekinah Glory*, also termed lightning and flaming fire.

5. In both the Olivet Discourse and 2 Thess, the unrepentant face eternal destruction.

6. And finally, in both there is a gathering together of those still alive and those who have been resurrected.

Since Jesus's teaching in the Olivet Discourse was the only New Testament scripture about end times available to the Apostle Paul, it isn't surprising that he used it as the basis for his epistle. These six comparisons in Chapter 1 make it obvious that Matt 24 was the source of Paul's inspiration.

But just like cresting a hill only to discover a beautiful hidden beach, when we begin to explore Chapter 2 of 1 Thess, there is even more. Much, much more.

> *For you yourselves know, brethren, that our coming to you was not in vain ... For our exhortation does not come from error or impurity or by way of deceit.* **(1 Thess 2:1, 3)**

Remember that this epistle is one continuous document. So when we begin to explore Chapter 2, it is really just a continuation of what we just looked at. And when Paul mentions the coming of the Lord and our gathering to Him — which is a reference to the rapture — he is speaking of what he just discussed only a few verses previously.

When Jesus comes in flaming fire, proponents of the Pre-Tribulation rapture theory have had to claim that this as a reference back to Paul's previous letter, 1 Thess. But looking at Chapters 1 and 2 of 2 Thess together clearly demonstrates how impossible their claim is. Paul is explaining further what he started out his letter talking about. It is a single, continuous message. And the subject was that the Thessalonians didn't need to be worried that they had missed the rapture, the gathering together.

Paul gave them the reason not to be worried. He told them that the rapture would not take place unless two signs are seen, as we have previously discussed. In this article we are going to prove this claim again, using different means. If Paul based his teaching in 2 Thess 2 on Matt 24, then we can safely say that the *concepts* come directly from Matt 24 — such as, what was the apostasy, and what is the timing of the revealing of Antichrist?

So let's look at the comparisons. There are an amazing *eleven more* identical comparisons:

1. Paul uses the same Greek word to describe Jesus's coming, *parousia*.

2. When Paul wanted to refer to the rapture, he didn't use the term from his previous letter but used the same exact Greek root word used in the Matt 24 rapture passage, *episunagoge*, or gather together.

3. Paul also begins his discussion with a passage about *not being deceived*, just as it was Jesus's first point in Matt 24.

4. One of the two signs that Paul said must precede the rapture is the *apostasy* or falling away. Jesus referred to this same event in Matt 24:10 as taking place during the Great Tribulation.

5. Paul and Jesus mentioned *lawlessness* that will prevail during the Great Tribulation, and again Paul uses the same exact Greek word for lawlessness as used in Matt 24: *anomia*.

6. Paul's second sign which must occur before the rapture is the *abomination of desolation*; and as we have learned, this is the most important sign for believers to know and recognize because, as Matt 24 informs us, it is after this sign that the Great Tribulation begins.

7. Both 2 Thess and Matt 24 refer to the abomination as occurring in the Holy Place, the Temple of God.

8. Paul refers to Matt 24 in naming the false Christ as the man of sin instrumental in the deception.

9. Both 2 Thess and Matt 24 refer to the great signs and wonders the Antichrist will do.

10. Matt 24 implies that the power of Antichrist will diminish at the appearing of Jesus after the sixth seal. 2 Thess explicitly mentions this.

11. Both 2 Thess and Matt 24 specifically state that the *elect* will not be misled. In Matt 24 they are called the elect; in 2 Thess they are called *chosen*.

In truth, Paul referred to Matt 24 *seventeen* times! To not accept that Paul based the first two Chapters of 2 Thess on Matt 24 is to be, in my opinion, close-minded.

And what are the implications of this brand-new understanding?

The Foundation of 2 Thessalonians

- That the apostasy of 2 Thess 2 happens during the Great Tribulation.

- That the rapture happens after the midpoint of the Tribulation.

- That Matt 24 is meant for Christians.

- That the elect found in Matt 24 are Christians.

- And, finally, that the rapture — or as Paul and Jesus call it the *gathering together* — happens in Matt 24:31 after the Great Tribulation.

All of this means that there is no Pre-Tribulation rapture. It is an open-and-shut case.

Article Eight

The One Sign of Jesus's Return That Everyone Needs to Know

I sincerely hope that you have taken the time to pray about what you've learned thus far in this series of articles, and that you have seriously considered the scriptural truths presented. If so, my prayer is that you are now convinced that the church *will* face the Great Tribulation and the Antichrist. Perhaps a new revelation has dawned for you. Perhaps it's the *Dawn of A New Day* in your own spiritual journey.

But even if you haven't changed your mind, that's okay. The biggest mistake we all make regarding the question of whether or not we will enter the Tribulation is to think that it's strictly a question of being right or wrong. It isn't! It's a question of whether or not we're *prepared*.

This is not a trivial issue. Jesus told us this will be the greatest and most widespread time of persecution and distress in history. When we consider the Holocaust, and then realize that the Great Tribulation will be worse, then it's not trivial at all. Let that sink in for a moment!

I like to think of the Great Tribulation as a Category 10 hurricane — a spiritual hurricane. One that we *must* prepare for. In 2017, super hurricane Irma was scheduled to hit Florida as the strongest hurricane in recorded history. At the time, an elderly woman was interviewed on television about what she was doing to prepare. She thought a moment and then said, "I've taken in my garbage cans." As strange as that may sound,

The One Sign of Jesus's Return That Everyone Needs to Know

that was the full extent of her preparation. Can you imagine! The greatest hurricane in history, and all she was doing to prepare was taking in her garbage cans!

As a Church, we will soon face the greatest challenge this world has ever known. But we haven't even begun to prepare. To aid us in that preparation, Jesus gave us about two dozen specific commands for that time period. If we look at the number of verses the scriptures devote to each topic, a large percentage are about a single issue: *Watching for the sign of the end of the age.*

The disciples asked Jesus about this sign directly, and it's the same question we have today:

> *"What will be the sign?"* **(Matt 24:3)**

Jesus did not avoid this question or say there is no sign of His return. No, He clearly told the disciples *exactly* what *would* be the signs and what would *not* be the signs. He first told them what the signs of the end would *not* be:

1. False prophets and messiahs

2. War

3. Rumors of war

4. Famines

5. Earthquakes

These are things that have occurred for thousands of years, and although they will happen at the end, they aren't the signs. This is *critically important*, because these are exactly the things many prophecy teachers focus on as signs. We know these things aren't signs because:

1. They are not unique

2. They are not specific

3. They are not clear

These things have been happening throughout history and will continue to happen right up until the time of Jesus's return. To be a true, *biblical sign*, it must be something that can't be missed, mistaken, or misunderstood. So Jesus gave the disciples, and us, exactly that type of sign — a sign that could not be mistaken or misunderstood.

So when we as Christians see the *abomination of desolation*, then we are to take action; we are to know *at that time* that Jesus's return is at most only three-and-a-half years away. Nothing else is truly a sign.

> *So when you see the abomination of desolation spoken of by the prophet Daniel, standing in the holy place (let the reader understand).* **(Matt 24:15-16)**

The Apostle Paul confirmed this sign in 2 Thess. Now, we have previously learned that the Antichrist will desecrate the newly built Temple of God and that this is *the* sign.

> *Let no one deceive you in any way. For the day will not come, unless the rebellion comes first, and the man of lawlessness is revealed, the son of destruction, who opposes and exalts himself against every so-called god or object of worship, so that he takes his seat in the temple*

> *of God, proclaiming himself to be God, proclaiming himself to be God.* **(2 Thess 2:3-4)**

And we have also learned that the coming of Jesus and the rapture cannot happen until this sign occurs. This sign is unique, specific, and clear. It is the sign that the Great Tribulation is about to begin and the *one sign all Christians need to be aware of* and to teach to others.

Unfortunately, American Christian culture has largely taught that there isn't a sign before Jesus's return, that the rapture can occur at any time. This theory is known as *imminence*. It is a popular but mistaken belief, with the potential for eternal consequences.

As we have stated several times, 2 Thess was written because Paul wanted to clear up a misconception that the Thessalonians had about the timing of the rapture. They were afraid that the persecution they were experiencing meant that they were living in the time of God's wrath — which meant they had been left behind during the rapture of the faithful. And because there had been no signs, that would also have meant that the rapture had been imminent.

Paul set the Thessalonians straight and rebuked the idea of imminence. Using the strongest possible language, he called it a deception.

> *Let no on deceive you in any way. For that day will not come, unless ...* **(2 Thess. 2:3)**

Paul informed the Thessalonians that there was *one reason* why they were wrong in thinking that they had missed the rapture. And that reason was that *no signs* had occurred. 2 Thess completely destroys the doctrine of imminence with regard to the timing of the rapture.

Let me state that again because it's profound. By destroying the theory of imminence, 2 Thess totally negates the Pre-Tribulation rapture position. Followers of the Pretribulation rapture may choose to believe that Jesus can come *at any time*. But we have shown this is just not so! In fact, this is confirmed in the end times teachings of *both* Jesus and Paul, where we are instructed over 35 times to watch, to see, to be observant, and to be alert. For what — if not for a sign?

> *Watch therefore and pray always.* **(Luke 21:36)**

To all of this you may respond with that common scripture passage, "No one knows the day or the hour." How can this statement be true if there is a sign required? Well, it's actually true that the rapture can occur on any day — as long as:

1. It occurs during the last three and a half years of the Tribulation, and

2. It occurs *after* the sign of the end of the age

So the rapture can occur on any day that meets these criteria. It just can't occur today or on any day until the required sign has appeared.

This phrase, "No one knows the day or the hour," is frequently misquoted. The problem is, that's *not* what the Bible says. The Bible actually says that, "No one knows *that* day and hour." This makes a huge difference! An eternal difference!

> *Concerning **that** day and hour, no one knows.* **(Matt 24:36)**

Grammatically, *that day* must refer to something Jesus said previously in Matt 24. Since Jesus said nothing about a Pre-Tribulation rapture, this famous verse cannot refer to a rapture before the Tribulation, not under any circumstances. It can only refer to the one significant day that Jesus mentioned in Matt 24:

That day will be the rapture. However, it will be a Pre-Wrath rapture, as described in Matt 24:31:

> *And he will send out his angels with a loud trumpet call, and they will gather his elect from the four winds, from one end of heaven to the* other (**Matt 24:31**)

So, to summarize, there *will be* signs before the return of Jesus, and the one that all Christians should watch for first is the *abomination of desolation.*

Now, why were both Jesus and Paul anxious that Christians not be deceived into believing the rapture could occur at any time without signs? Simply because if Christians miss *this* sign, they may not be able to identify the Antichrist or the beginning of the Great Tribulation. Imagine the danger of not knowing that the Antichrist has appeared on the world scene or that it's his mark that will lead to eternal damnation!

You may wonder if there is anything you can do once you have seen this sign. Or you might even be interested in knowing if there are things you can do to prepare right now. Well, it just so happens that included within the pages of this book are several articles that address some things which you might consider doing. And for more information on how specifically to prepare for the last days, please look for my recently published book entitled — guess what — *How to Prepare for the Last Days*.

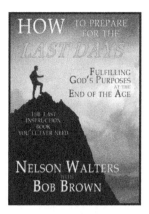 

Figure 8-1

Also, if you have a desire to learn more about the different rapture theories, please consider checking out my book on *Simplifying The Rapture*.

All of us — regardless what our opinion is regarding the chances that Christians will enter the Great Tribulation — need to prepare our churches and our families as if the chances of that occurring were 100%. Failing to do so may be the biggest mistake we ever make, one with eternally devastating consequences.

Article Nine

Was Matthew 24 Meant Solely for the Jews?

Are many — possibly even a majority — of our churches unintentionally disobeying the Great Commission? That's a pretty heavy question that we will explore in this article. And our study will be focused on one chapter of the Bible — Matt 24. But before we begin this discussion, let's first address the great enigma that this chapter represents.

Matt 24 describes events that happen during Daniel's 70th week, or as some like to call it, *the Tribulation*. And if this chapter pertains to the Church then, quite frankly, there is no Pre-Tribulation rapture — because Pre-Tribulationists believe the Church will be raptured *before* the Tribulation. But we have already proven that the Church *will* endure that period. On the other hand, if Matt 24 was only meant for unsaved Jews, then this would be defacto evidence for a Pre-Tribulation rapture. A lot rides on the answer to this enigma.

As we begin our discussion of this question, it's important to point out that Matt 24 *is* for the unsaved Jews; it's just not for them exclusively. God doesn't prohibit the unsaved — of any race or religion — from learning of His Word. The question really is this: Is the message of Matt 24 also for the Church? The Great Commission is, surprisingly, one of the things that will help us answer that question. This probably comes as a surprise to most who view the Great Commission strictly in terms of evangelism. But it's so much more than that.

Immediately prior to Jesus's ascension into heaven, He instructed all Christians on what they were to do in His absence:

Was Matthew 24 Meant Solely for the Jews?

> *Go therefore and make disciples of all the nations, baptizing them in the name of the Father and the Son and the Holy Spirit, teaching them to observe all that I commanded you; and lo, I am with you always, even to the end of the age.* **(Matt 28:19-20)**

Most of us are, or should be, familiar with this passage. It provides us with four commands, and a promise:

1. The first command is to *go* (the literal Greek is *as you are going*).

2. As we are going, we are to *make disciples*.

3. And we are to *baptize them*.

4. And we are to *teach them* to obey *all* Jesus commanded.

Jesus then gave them, and us, *a promise* that He would be with His church until a specific event, known as *the end of the age.*

The first three commands are well understood and are preached from nearly every pulpit in the world on Sunday mornings. So we are only going to focus on the fourth command and the promise. It is this final instruction, teaching *all* that Jesus commanded, where the Church is deficient. *All* means *everything*! Every chapter in the New Testament and every command.

So, to say a certain section of the New Testament isn't for Christians and is only for unsaved Jews is to disobey the Great Commission, by failing to teach *all* that Jesus commanded, to *all* nations — including 12 specific commands in Matt 24. And as if to reinforce this meaning, Jesus adds the promise that He will be with us to the *end of the age*.

The concept of the *end of the age* is the subject of the parable of the wheat and the tares in Matt 13. In that parable, Jesus told us that the end of the age is the *harvest*, the separation of the righteous from the un-righteous. At that time the un-righteous will be burned with fire. This is *not* a Pre-Tribulation event. Even the staunchest Pre-Tribulation scholars believe that this happens near the end of the Tribulation.

Jesus said in Matt 28 that He would be with His Church up until this event. In fact, the Greek words translated *always* actually means *all the days*. So, Jesus will be with His Church *all the days*, until the wicked are burned with fire. As we stated earlier, this precludes a Pre-Tribulation rapture, as Jesus is present with the Church up until this point.

Let's return now to Matt 24 and see how it's related to this term, *the end of the age*. Jesus's discussion in Matt 24 is the result of a question the disciples asked: They wanted to know the sign of this specific event, *the end of the age*:

> *What will be the sign of Your coming, and of the end of the age?* **(Matt. 24:3)**

And Jesus gave them the sign:

> *Immediately after the tribulation of those days the sun will be darkened, and the moon will not give its light, and the stars will fall from heaven.* **(Matt. 24:29)**

As we see, the sign is the darkening of the sun and moon and the falling of the stars. Jesus told us the sign happens *after* the Great Tribulation. That is when *the end of the age* and the *harvest*

Was Matthew 24 Meant Solely for the Jews?

occur. And Jesus promised to be with His church up until that day.

We see, therefore, that the Great Commission and Matt 24 are intimately linked, with the Great Commission providing two powerful pieces of evidence that Matt 24 is for the Church:

1. That Jesus will be with His church throughout the entirety of Matt 24, all the days until the end of the age.

2. That we are to teach all of Jesus's special commands for that period of time in our churches.

We also find that there is a specific group mentioned in Matt 24: The *elect*, which means *those that are chosen*. Most Pre-Tribulation supporters claim that this term refers to unsaved Jews, because the Greek *Old Testament* uses this word to refer to Jews. However, in the *New Testament*, this word is *never* used to refer to unsaved Jews; and in all cases but two, it refers to Christians.

In Matt 24, the Greek word translated *the elect* is used three times:

1. In verse 22, we see that the days of the Great Tribulation will be cut short for this group, *the elect*, and it will be cut short for them only:

    Unless those days had been cut short, no life would have been saved; but for the sake of the elect those days will be cut short. **(Matt 24:22)**

2. In verse 24, we see that the Antichrist and the false prophet will deceive unbelievers with great signs and miracles; he'll deceive everyone *except the elect.*

   For false Christs and false prophets will arise and will show great signs and wonders, so as to mislead, if possible, even the elect. **(Matt 24:24)**

3. And finally, in verse 31, the *gathering together*, which we now know is the rapture, is a gathering of these same *elect*.

   And He will send forth His angels with a great trumpet and they will gather together His elect from the four winds, from one end of the sky to the other. **(Matt 24:31)**

Now, let's look at the second verse in more detail:

For false Christs and false prophets will arise and will show great signs and wonders, so as to mislead, if possible, even the elect. **(Matt 24:24)**

Notice that the Antichrist's deception is so great that he would have deceived *even the elect*, except that deceiving them is impossible. Now is that what we believe about national Israel and the unsaved Jews? No. Nearly all Christians expect Jews to be deceived by the Antichrist — after all, aren't these the same people who got it wrong when Christ came the first time? Many assume that they will make a covenant with him, as well. So *the elect* can't be unsaved Jews, can they? No, because Israel will be deceived.

Additionally, there is amazing evidence that the early church believed that the words *the elect* in Matthew 24 were specifically understood to be the Church. In the *Didache*, a first century document which is thought by most to be a collection of the sayings of the Apostles, we find a quote from Matt 24:31 — probably the most important use of *the elect* in the New Testament. But notice the word used in the Didache for *those gathered from the four winds:* It's *Church*!

> *Remember, Lord, your Church, to save her from every evil, and to perfect her in your love, and to gather her together from the four winds.* **(Didache 10:5)**

The compilers of the Didache did not use the word *elect*. It is obvious that the compilers of the Didache, or perhaps the Apostles themselves, believed that *the elect* were the Church, and that these terms were interchangeable.

From all this, we must conclude that *the elect* in Matt 24 are the Church. And if they are the Church, then *they* are the ones *gathered together* or raptured after the Great Tribulation.

So what possible response is there to this overwhelming evidence? What could possibly support the assertion that Matt 24 is only for unsaved Jews and cause us to disobey the Great Commission? When you hear it you'll say, "Really, that's all?"

> *Then those who are in Judea must flee to the mountain. Whoever is on the housetop must not go down to get the things out that are in his house. Whoever is in the field must not turn back to get his cloak. But woe to those who are pregnant and to those who are nursing babies in those days! But pray that your flight will not be in the winter, or on a Sabbath.* **(Matt 24:16-20)**

Pre-Tribulation rapture proponents claim that the mention of the Hebraic terms *Sabbath* and *Judea* in Matt 24 is the proof that this chapter is *only* for the Jews. It hardly is. First, Judea is mentioned not because it's a Hebraic term, but because it's the epicenter of the Antichrist's Great Tribulation; he sits down in the Temple at the abomination of desolation in Judea, today's West Bank. And it makes sense that those who are there should evacuate first. Second, both *Sabbath* and *winter* are mentioned because these are times when it would be difficult to evacuate. Travel is difficult in winter, and during the Sabbath large numbers of observant Jews block the highways in and out of Jerusalem.

If we were going to say that the terms *Judea* and *Sabbath* indicate that Matt 24 is only for the Jews, we could just as easily say that the inclusion of *winter* and *pregnancy* would indicate that it is only for expectant mothers from Wisconsin. Both ideas are nonsense. *Judea* and *Sabbath* are mentioned for the same reason that Jesus might mention *winter* and *pregnancy* – for practical reasons.

In conclusion, Jesus instructed us to teach His followers all that He commanded. In my opinion, that includes the commands found in Matt 24. So, is a large portion of the church disobeying the Great Commission, and is Matt 24 meant specifically for Christians? I believe the overwhelming evidence says *yes* to both.

Article Ten

Will the Rapture be Visible or Invisible?

Will Jesus's coming be visible or invisible? Will it be a secret rapture, where only the saints see Him, but no one else? Or will everyone see Him? Let's explore these issues in this article.

I'm sure you've heard about the rapture being secret or invisible, that *in a twinkling of an eye* every saved person on earth will disappear, leaving behind nothing but a pile of empty clothing. Yes, we've probably all heard that idea. But where is it found in the Bible? Well, truth be told, it's not in the Bible at all.

The phrase *twinkling of an eye* is itself biblical. It's found in 1 Cor 15:

> *Behold, I tell you a mystery; we will not all sleep, but we will all be changed, in a moment, in the twinkling of an eye, at the last trumpet; for the trumpet will sound, and the dead will be raised imperishable, and we will be changed.* **(1 Cor 15:51-52)**

Looking at this passage carefully, we see that it is about the things that happens just before the rapture. The last trumpet is blown, and the dead are raised to life. Both of these things happen right before the rapture, as we see in the most famous rapture passage in the Bible, 1 Thess 4:16-17:

> *For the Lord Himself will descend from heaven with a shout, with the voice of the archangel and with the trumpet of God, and the dead in Christ will rise first. Then we who are alive and remain will be caught up*

Will the Rapture be Visible or Invisible?

together with them in the clouds to meet the Lord in the air, and so we shall always be with the Lord. **(1 Thess 4:16-17)**

So, the logic goes that if the rapture happens in the twinkling of an eye, unbelievers won't have time to see Jesus; but once believers reach the clouds, they'll see Jesus. According to this theory, *unbelievers* won't see Jesus at the rapture, but *believers* will. And that's what makes the twinkling of an eye verse the most quoted biblical support for the theory that Jesus will be invisible at the rapture.

Surprisingly, even one of the most popular online Christian organizations, *GotQuestions.org*, openly claims that "the rapture is *secret* in that no one will see Jesus coming except believers."

And there are other supporters of this position, as well:

- Dr. Ed Hindson, Dean of Liberty University's School of Divinity, and co-author Pastor Mark Hitchcock's recent book, *Can We Still Believe in the Rapture*, uses the 1 Cor 15 passage to support an instantaneous and invisible return of Jesus.

- Pastor Robert Jeffress, of *Pathway to Victory*, a prominent radio and TV ministry, also says 1 Cor 15 supports that Jesus's coming will be in the twinkling of an eye.

- And, of course, the late Pastor Tim LaHaye, and his co-author Jerry Jenkins, used this exact phrase, *in a twinkling of an eye*, in the title of their book about the rapture.

So, if all of these organizations, pastors, and even Deans of divinity schools have claimed that this passage says Jesus is invisible at the rapture, then He must be. Right?

Maybe not. The phrase *twinkling of an eye* certainly is in the verse. But what is it that actually happens in a moment, in a twinkling of an eye?

The verse actually says that we will *all be changed* in the twinkling of an eye. *That* is what happens quickly, at the sound of the last trumpet. First, the trumpet will sound. Second, the dead in Christ will be raised and given imperishable bodies. And third, the living will all be changed into similar imperishable bodies. But where is the rapture in this passage? Do you see it? I don't see it. Where is the *catching up*, the Greek term *harpazo?* Where is the *gathering together* to Him or the *meeting Jesus in the air?* None of those things, typically associated with the rapture, are found in this passage. So the rapture isn't found in this passage, either.

No one argues that those things (the resurrection and the change into resurrection bodies) don't take place right before the rapture. They do. If we look again at 1 Thess. 4, we see these same things. First, there is the trumpet. And second, the dead in Christ will rise. The order is the same in 1 Thess 4 and 1 Cor 15. But 1 Thess 4 is specific that the rapture *only* takes place *after* these preliminary events. It uses the term *then*, and only after that transitional word do we see terms about the rapture, like *catching up, gathering together,* and *meeting the Lord in the air.*

So, there are two phases to the rapture. In the first phase, the trumpet blows, the dead in Christ rise, and we are all changed. This preliminary phase is the one that happens in *a twinkling of an eye*. Only after this are the resurrected and those who have

Will the Rapture be Visible or Invisible?

been changed caught up together into the air to meet Jesus. But the Bible is *unclear* how long this second phase of the rapture takes. Might the rapture take considerably *longer* than a twinkling of an eye?

> *And after He had said these things, He was lifted up while they were looking on, and a cloud received Him out of their sight. And as they were gazing intently into the sky while He was going, behold, two men in white clothing stood beside them.* **(Acts 1:9-10)**

When Jesus ascended into heaven — which Rev 12:5 refers to as a rapture, or *harpazo* — the disciples watched Him as He was lifted up. This implies a longer period than a moment. Doesn't it stand to reason that if Jesus took longer than a moment to be raptured, then so will the saints? And the rapture will certainly be a noisy event. There will be a shout, there is a trumpet, and there is the voice of the archangel. Although nothing is said here about seeing Jesus, it's certainly going to be an attention-getting event.

Although the idea of an instantaneous, invisible rapture seems like a biblical fact to many, when we put it under the magnifying glass of God's Word, we learn that it probably is a myth. So how did the idea of an invisible return of Jesus originate?

John Nelson Darby, who codified the concepts of the Pre-Tribulation rapture in the early 1800's, came up with the idea. But why did he specify that the appearing of Jesus had to be invisible? Why did he come up with this idea, especially if it isn't found in the Bible?

Dr. Thomas Ice, Director of the Pre-Tribulation Research Center, and probably the leading scholar on the Pre-Tribulation rapture position, gives us the answer. In a 2018 email from Dr. Ice to a friend, he admitted that the invisible return of Jesus isn't found in scripture but, rather, is a "contrastive deduction," or a presumption. He stated that since Rev 1:7 indicates that every eye will see Him *after* the beginning of the Tribulation period it can't be referring to a Pre-Tribulation rapture. In his mind, there must therefore be two appearance of Jesus: An invisible, Pre-Tribulation appearance, and a later, visible appearance. He claims that this is the same deduction that Darby made and for the same reason.

But does this deduction stand up to scrutiny? Both Dr. Ice and Darby are using a theory not explicitly stated in the Bible — the Pre-Tribulation rapture theory — to prove another theory not found in the Bible — the invisible return of Jesus theory. Am I the only one who sees this as a logical fallacy — using one un-truth to prove another un-truth?

But there is more evidence than just logic to disprove the invisible return theory. There are approximately 50 passages in the Bible about the return of Jesus, and Dr. Ice has concluded that 13 of them are about the visual appearing of Jesus to *only* the saints at a Pre-Tribulation rapture. These are passages that include the words *appearing, revealing* or *seeing* in regard to Jesus's return. During these appearing events, the saints receive glorified bodies or are made eternally righteous, things that only happen at the rapture.

However, there are three problems with these passages being about an invisible return:

Will the Rapture be Visible or Invisible?

First, all the terms — like appear, appearing, and revealing — are *singular*, implying that there is one, and only one, end times appearing, not two. And if that isn't enough, there isn't one of these 13 visual appearance of Jesus that in any way qualifies as an appearing to only the saints. Think about it: If there were truly two end times appearances, as Dr. ice claims, don't you think a couple of them would make it clear that they were an appearing to the righteous or an appearing to *only* the saints, in order to differentiate that event from the other appearing?. But not one of the 13 passages does this. Let that sink in. Thirteen passages all use the singular, as in only one of something; and none of them qualify this in any way, to eliminate the possibility of confusion. That makes no sense to me. How about you?

Second, two of the passages specifically preclude an invisible appearing. This passage from Heb 9 recalls that there was an appearing of Jesus in the first century:

> *So Christ also, having been offered once to bear the sins of many will appear a second time for salvation without reference to sin, to those who eagerly await Him.* **(Heb 9:28)**

And there will be a *second appearing - in* the end times. If there was an extra, third appearing, as Pre-Tribulation proponents suppose, wouldn't the Bible mention this? After all, this passage is specifically about the appearings of Jesus.

In another passage about Jesus's end times appearing found in 1 John, we see that the reader is instructed to abide in Jesus:

> *Now, little children, abide in Him, so that when He appears, we may have confidence and not shrink away from Him in shame at His coming ... Beloved,*

> *now we are children of God, and it has not appeared as yet what we will be. We know that when He appears, we will be like Him, because we will see Him just as He is.*
> **(1 John 2:28, 3:2)**

In John's gospel, Jesus told us that only those who abide in Him are true believers. Others, who don't abide in Him, are cut off from the vine and burned. They are unbelievers. And this passage from 1 John is obviously talking about the rapture, because it speaks of Christians being made like Jesus. At His appearing, they will be given resurrection bodies.

However, we also learn that those who don't abide in Jesus — the non-believers — will shrink back from Jesus in shame at this appearing. How can they do that if they don't see Him? Think about that for a moment! No one shrinks back or hides from someone's appearing if they can't see Him. So, in this passage we see two word-for-word references to the appearing of Jesus — a *singular* appearing.

Yet in this one and only appearing, non-believers see Jesus and hide from Him in shame, while believers receive glorified bodies. In this one appearance, we find that the righteous are given resurrection bodies, and the un-righteous see Jesus. That doesn't sound like an invisible return at all!

Let's summarize. First, we have learned that the invisible return of Jesus isn't biblical. Second, we have unfortunately also learned that a majority of Pre-Tribulation leaders wrongly cite 1 Cor 15:51-52 as proof that it is. Be on the alert for this erroneous citation. Third, we have learned from Dr. Thomas Ice that the idea of an invisible return of Jesus was manufactured, having evolved as a deduction by John Darby. And, finally, we have

Will the Rapture be Visible or Invisible?

used other scriptures, like 1 John 2, to disprove the idea completely.

Article Eleven

Is Matthew 24:31 the Rapture or the Second Coming?

In Article 9 we rather definitively determined that Matt 24 is not meant solely for unsaved Jews, but rather, is meant primarily for Christians. I'm sure that conclusion left a lot of you with questions in your mind. Specifically, you may have wondered about verses 29-31:

> *But immediately after the tribulation of those days the sun will be darkened, and the moon will not give off its light, and the stars will fall from the sky, and the powers of the heavens will be shaken. And then the sign of the Son of Man will appear in the sky, and then all the tribes of the earth will mourn, and they will see the son of man coming on the clouds of the sky with power and great glory, And He will send forth His angels with a great trumpet and they will gather together His elect from the four winds, from one end of the sky to the other.* **(Matt 24:29-31)**

You might be asking, "Isn't this passage about the Second Coming? Why do you keep calling it the rapture?"

Ninety-nine percent of the church has been taught that this passage refers to what our culture calls the Second Coming, when Jesus mounts a white horse and returns to fight the Battle of Armageddon. But as we look at the Matt 24 passage carefully:

- We don't see Jesus on a white horse. Rather, we see Him coming on the clouds.

Is Matthew 24:31 the Rapture or the Second Coming?

- We don't see Him leading or fighting a battle. Rather, we see Him sending His angels to gather the elect.

However, when we compare Matt 24 to 1 Thess. 4-5 — the traditional rapture passage — we see all kinds of *similarities*. So, the issue is really this: *What event is Matt 24:29-31?* Is it the rapture, or is it Christ's Second Coming?

Before we answer that question, let's examine the chronology of end times events. Both the Pre-Tribulation rapture theory and the Pre-Wrath rapture theory envision two events:

1. A rapture when Jesus returns to gather together His elect into heaven.

2. And then a separate, second event: The physical return of Jesus to the earth to fight the Battle of Armageddon.

Both theories place the physical return of Jesus at the very end of the Tribulation. Both suppose that Rev 19:11-15 depicts this event. Both theories also believe 1 Thess 4-5 depicts the rapture. And both imagine it occurring before the wrath of God, although they do differ on the timing, which you can learn more about by reading Article 3: *Will Christians Face the Great Tribulation?*

However, the theories dramatically differ on what event Matt 24:29-31 represents. The Pre-Tribulation rapture theory assumes that the Matt 24 passage is the same event as the Rev 19 passage, and that it happens at the end of the Tribulation.

The Pre-Wrath rapture theory assumes that Matt 24 is the same event as 1 Thess 4-5, and that both occur sometime after the middle of the tribulation, prior to the wrath of God and perhaps a year from the end, as represented in Figure 11-1:

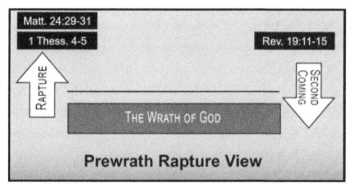

Figure 11-1

This difference of opinion between the two theories is significant. Very significant. Because Matt 24:29-31 occurs *after* the Great Tribulation. By definition, if this passage is the same as 1 Thess 4-5 and neither are the same as Rev 19, then there can be *no Pre-Tribulation rapture.* Period! Let me state that again, because it's very important: If Matt 24:29-31 is proven to be the same as 1 Thess 4-5 — in other words, is proven to depict the rapture — or, if it's proven to *not* be the same as Rev 19 — which we call the Second Coming — then there can be *no* Pre-Tribulation rapture. This is because the gathering together in Matt 24 has to come *after* the Great Tribulation. That makes this the *most definitive proof* in this series of articles.

Let's begin our inquiry by looking at the similarities and differences between these passages: 1 Thess 4-5, Rev 19:11-15, and Matt 24:29-31. And throughout this inquiry, remember that if Matt 24 is proven to be the same as 1 Thess 4-5 or *not* the same as Rev 19, then there is no Pre-Tribulation rapture, by definition.

Is Matthew 24:31 the Rapture or the Second Coming?

Here are 10 points to consider:

1. Matt 24 is called a coming, or *parousia* in Greek. In fact, Matt 24 uses this term four times. 1 Thess uses this term as well; but Rev 19 does not. In both Matt and Thess the word *coming* is singular and includes the definitive article, *the*. In both cases, it is the one and *only* coming. In fact, every use of this term in the New Testament is singular; there can't be two comings, only one. And *if there is only one, by definition Matt 24 and 1 Thess. are the same thing.* We could stop right here and claim to have proven our point, but there is much more to discover!

2. 1 Thess refers to a resurrection, and Rev 19 doesn't. But, does Matt 24 refer to a resurrection? At first, you'd think it doesn't, but let's examine it more closely. When Jesus described the Great Tribulation, He was actually quoting the prophet Daniel. And this passage from Daniel *does* include the resurrection. So when Jesus referred to Dan 12:1, He referred to everything that went with that verse, including Dan 12:2, which includes the resurrection. Matt 24 *does* mention the resurrection, if only by reference:

For then there will be great tribulation, such as has not been from the beginning of the world until now, no, and never will be. **(Matt 24:21)**

And there shall be a time of trouble, such as never has been since there was a nation till that time. **(Dan 12:1)**

> *But at that time your people shall be delivered, everyone whose name shall be found written in the book. And many of those who sleep in the dust of the earth shall awake, some to everlasting life.* **(Dan 12:1-2)**

3. Both Matt 24 and 1 Thess liken Jesus's return to birth pangs, but Rev 19 does not.

4. Both Matt 24 and 1 Thess have the presence of angels, but Rev 19 does not.

5. Both Matt 24 and 1 Thess refer to sinners as drunk, but Rev 19 does not.

6. Both Matt 24 and 1 Thess have a trumpet, but Rev 19 does not. In Rev 19, Jesus actually has a sword in His mouth, which precludes Him from blowing a trumpet — which Zech 9:14 specifically states is blown by Jesus on that day.

7. Both Matt 24 and 1 Thess depict Jesus coming on the clouds, but Rev 19 does not. In fact, in Rev 19 He comes on a horse.

8. Both Matt 24 and 1 Thess depict a gathering together of the elect, but Rev 19 does not.

9. In 1 Thess and in Mark's nearly identical version of the gathering together (Mark 13), the direction of the saints is up; but in Rev 19 the saints return with Jesus in a downward direction.

10. Finally, in a very crucial point of comparison, we find that in 1 Thess and Matt 24 the timing of Jesus's return is unknown (we are told Jesus comes

Is Matthew 24:31 the Rapture or the Second Coming?

like a thief); but in Rev 19, it is completely known: It comes three-and-a-half years after the abomination of desolation.

I liken this comparison to the classic children's game, *One Of These Is Not Like The Others*. The difference between Rev 19 and the other two passages — as we have shown — is like comparing apples to oranges. Matt 24 and 2 Thess are alike in 10 important ways; and just as importantly, they are *not* like Rev 19.

There are several other ways that Matt 24 cannot be the same event as Rev 19, and these are critically important. If Matt 24 isn't the physical Second Coming, not only is the Pre-Tribulation rapture theory disproven, but so are the Mid-Tribulation and Post-Tribulation positions, all of which depend upon Matt 24:31 occurring at the end of the Tribulation Period.

Every one of these theories must now ask the question, "If Matt 24 is *not* the same as Rev 19, then what is it?" The answer, of course, is that Matt 24:31 is the rapture.

There are several other critical, insurmountable differences, as well:

- In Matt 24, the un-repentant are taken by complete surprise — just as in the days of Noah. In Rev 19 there is no surprise; in fact, Satan, the Antichrist, and the false prophet begin to gather the armies of the earth, prior to Jesus's return, in order to fight against Him.

- In Matt 24, none of the trumpet and bowl judgments are referenced. In Matt 24, Jesus is giving us signs of His coming, and it is universally accepted that Matt 24 depicts the first six seals in exact order. Why then would Jesus exclude the trumpet and bowls? The answer is that they are the wrath of God and come *after* the rapture. Therefore, Jesus has no need to mention them. The Rev 19 passage, however, comes after all the trumpet and bowl judgments and is, in fact, the seventh bowl. This will probably shock everyone, but there is no fiery judgment pictured in Rev 19! However, the first trumpet *is* a fiery judgment, and it falls exactly where the Pre-Wrath rapture predicts — right after the opening of the seals and Matt 24.

So, in all of these amazing ways, we have proven that 1 Thess 4 — the *only* passage in the Bible that Pre-Tribulation proponents can possibly claim is supporting a Pre-Tribulation rapture — is actually the same as Matt 24:29-31. We have also proven that Rev 19 — where Jesus rides a white horse — is not the same as Matt 24. Only a Pre-Wrath rapture is consistent with all of these amazing proofs.

Article Twelve

Was the Flood a Picture of the Coming of the Wrath of God?

Everyone has a theory about when the wrath of God occurs and how long it will be. But you will probably be shocked to learn what the Bible says about this. It is probably not the answer you expect or have heard before. So let's start at the beginning, at pretty much the beginning of everything, and ask our question: Was the flood a picture of the coming wrath of God?

But before we go there, let's talk about what the Bible says about the day of wrath, on which God will pour out His judgment on the un-repentant. No New Testament book has more to say about the wrath of God than the book of Romans:

> *But because of your hard and impenitent heart you are storing up wrath for yourself on the day of wrath when God's righteous judgment will be revealed.* **(Rom 2:5)**

Now this is an uncomfortable topic for some. Why would a righteous and loving God inflict His wrath?

> *"(Is) God is un-righteous to inflict wrath on us? (I speak in a human way.) By no means! For then how could God judge the world?"* **(Rom. 3:5-6)**

Certainly, there are those fully deserving of God's wrath — those prone to the vileness of human trafficking, drugs, terrorism, murder, torture, and abuse of all kinds deserve God's judgment. Why would God *not* bring an end to such things and judge those responsible?

Was the Flood a Picture of the Coming of the Wrath of God?

The short answer is that He will. But even those who are doing these vile acts have been given time to repent — for a time. Right up until the time that God says, "Enough!"

> *The Lord is not slow to fulfill his promise as some count slowness, but is patient toward you, not wishing that any should perish, but that all should reach repentance. But the day of the Lord will come like a thief, and then the heavens will pass away with a roar, and the heavenly bodies will be burned up and dissolved, and the earth and the works that are done on it will be exposed.* **(2 Pet 3:9-10)**

God has promised that He will save those justified by the blood of the Messiah Jesus before His wrath is poured out, even those who have seriously transgressed His wishes:

> *Since, therefore, we have now been justified by his blood, much more shall we be saved by him from the wrath of God.* **(Rom 5:9)**

So we know the wrath of God is coming. But how long will it be, and what will it be like? Everyone has a theory. Some people say the wrath of God lasts the entire seven years of the 70th Week of Daniel. Others say it is a single day, the *Day of the Lord*. But what does the Bible say?

Not surprisingly the Bible has a very consistent answer. But it is probably not the answer that you think it is. Maybe not even the answer you want it to be. A good place to begin is at the beginning, and Genesis is the book of beginnings. In that book God poured out His wrath for the first time in the flood. Peter tells us that the flood was a picture of the wrath to come:

> *The world that then existed was deluged with water*

> *and perished. But by the same word the heavens and earth that now exist are stored up for fire, being kept until the day of judgment and destruction of the ungodly.* **(2 Pet 3:6-7)**

Peter tells us that the world is currently being protected or kept, but a day is coming when fire will destroy it and the ungodly, much as water did then.

Jesus tells us this exact same thing:

> *For as the lightning flashes and lights up the sky from one side to the other, so will the Son of Man be in his day . . . Just as it was in the days of Noah, so will it be in the days of the Son of Man. They were eating and drinking and marrying and being given in marriage, until the day when Noah entered the ark, and the flood came and destroyed them all.* **(Luke 17:24, 26-27)**

> *Likewise, just as it was in the days of Lot – they were eating and drinking, buying and selling, planting and building, but on the day when Lot went out from Sodom, fire and sulfur rained from heaven and destroyed them all – so will it be on the day when the Son of Man is revealed.* **(Luke 17:28-30)**

So we see that Jesus uses two, back-to-back accounts from Genesis to explain the coming wrath of God for us, the account of the flood and the account of the destruction of Sodom and Gomorrah. Jesus tells us His wrath will be like that. It will be like Noah's *flood*, but it will involve *fire* like Sodom.

Let's look at Jesus's words closely, because there is a lot of information stored up in them. First, notice that, in both of the two accounts, the un-righteous who will be destroyed will be

Was the Flood a Picture of the Coming of the Wrath of God?

doing a number of things right up until the very day of judgment: *Eating and drinking, marrying and being given in marriage, buying and selling, planting and building.* In essence, Jesus is saying the un-righteous will be living totally normal lives before the wrath of God is poured out in the form of fire and brimstone that comes upon them suddenly.

Is that what you've been taught? My guess is probably not. You were most likely taught that Jesus returns like lightning, that fire and brimstone fall on the last day of the 70th Week, and that the Second Coming happens at the end — after all the seals, trumpets and bowls. Does that sound more like what you've been taught?

But Jesus tells us that the un-righteous will be living normal lives when those things happen, when Jesus returns like lightning and the fire starts falling. Well, I'm sorry, but it's impossible for those things to happen on the last day. Just think about it.

There's no way the un-righteous — or anybody for that matter — will be living normal lives at that point in history. Before the end, the trumpet judgments have to blow. And during the trumpets, one-third of the vegetation on earth will be burned; one-third of the water supplies will be made bitter; demonic locusts will sting the inhabitants of the earth for five straight months, causing them to seek death but not find it; and one-third of the population of the world will perish in fire and brimstone.

Can you imagine building and planting during those events? Or getting married? No, that doesn't make any sense at all. No one would build a house while fire and brimstone are falling or plant while the trees and grass are being burned up. Those things that we consider normal life can only take place *before* the trumpets are sounded.

So, here is a clue from Jesus: He returns like lightning, where every eye sees Him, and the wrath happens — all *prior to* a single trumpet judgment. It's the only way the scriptures make sense. And, given time, the scriptures *always* make sense.

Remember, the fifth trumpet alone is five months long:

> *They were allowed to torment them for five months.* **(Rev 9:5)**

The trumpets have to blow at least five months before the last day. So Jesus's return in the sky as lightning from one end the earth to the other must happen *at least* 5 months prior to the end of the 70th Week. But how much earlier? If we look at the events of the first flood, perhaps we can get a clue.

I first became aware of this all of in a wonderful book by my good friends Dr. Joseph Lenard and Donald Zoller, entitled *The Last Shofar!* In that book, the authors calculate the exact number of days Noah was in the ark during the flood.

In Genesis, God's word tells us precisely when Noah entered the ark:

> *In the six hundredth year of Noah's life in the second month, on the seventeenth day of the month, on that day all the fountains of the great deep burst forth.* **(Gen 7:11)**

And it also tells us when Noah left the ark:

Was the Flood a Picture of the Coming of the Wrath of God?

> *In the six hundred and first year, ... In the second month, on the twenty-seventh day of the month, the earth had dried out. Then God said to Noah, "Go out from the ark."* **(Gen 8:13-16)**

So, Noah was in the ark exactly one year and 10 days. Why does God give us this precise timing? If this is how long the *first* wrath of God lasted, is it possible that this is also how long the coming wrath of God by fire and brimstone will last? That is our theory — that it will be *one year and ten days long.*

Let's see what else the Bible has to say about this. Are there passages in the Bible that seem to indicate that the wrath will be about a year long? Not surprisingly, there are:

> *For the Lord has a day of vengeance, a year of recompense for the cause of Zion.* **(Isa 34:8)**

I'm guessing that this is probably new to you. You may have read this before, but you likely never gave it much thought. It says that God has a day of vengeance, and that His recompense, or pay back, for what the un-repentant did to Zion will take *an entire year.*

Now that is one witness. Are there any more?

> *For the day of vengeance was in my heart, and my year of redemption had come.* **(Isa 63:4)**

Again the day of vengeance is associated with a year-long period. This time it's a year when God will accomplish a redemption, as well.

Are there any more? Yes!

> *To proclaim the acceptable year of the Lord, and the day of vengeance of our God; to comfort all who mourn.* **(Isa 61:2)**

This one was quoted by Jesus, at least in part, during His ministry.

So there are now 3 separate passages that associate the day of vengeance, the Day of the Lord, with a year-long period of time. And three things happen in this year: Recompense, or payback; redemption; and the determination that the year be an *acceptable* year. We will explore these 3 things in more depth in a moment.

But first let's look at another example that sets aside a year as a special time period, this time from the book of Daniel:

> *And he shall make a strong covenant with many for one week.* **(Dan 9:27)**

"Okay," you're probably saying, "Daniel mentions seven years, not one." And that is absolutely true. However, this seven-year period is known as a *shabua*, or a *seven-year sabbatical cycle of seven years*. All 70 of Daniel's weeks are seven-year sabbatical cycles, or weeks of years.

But a *week of years* is not just some random period of seven years. It's called a week because there is an organization to this week of years:

> *Keep a Sabbath to the Lord. For six years you shall sow your field, and for six years you shall prune your vineyard and gather in its fruits, but in the seventh year there shall be a Sabbath of solemn rest for the land, a Sabbath to the Lord. You shall not sow your field or prune your vineyard.* **(Lev 25:2-4)**

Was the Flood a Picture of the Coming of the Wrath of God?

We learn here that the final year of the sabbatical cycle is different than the first six. And Daniel's 70th weeks is just like that. The final year of the 70th Week is different from the first six!! So let's explore it a little more.

This week of years is modeled on the Lord's week of days, six days of toil and a Sabbath that is set aside for God's people to rest. Daniel's 70th Week is exactly like that. Six years of toil where God's people sow and reap a harvest of souls, and a separate year of rest. And the final year is different than the first six. It is our opinion that this year is the *acceptable year* of recompense and redemption, as seen in Isaiah.

Now that we've seen all these examples from the Old Testament, let's look at the three things that happen in that final year of Daniel's 70th Week:

1. First comes recompense, or payback, for the cause of Zion. During the Tribulation period, the Antichrist and his kingdom are going to occupy the Temple and persecute God's people. The final year is Jesus's payback, His wrath. This will start with the trumpet judgments.

2. It is also a year of redemption. Who will be redeemed during this year? The unsaved Jews, primarily. It will be a year when they, and some Gentiles, come to faith in Jesus.

3. Finally, it is the *acceptable year* of the Lord. What does this mean? It means that we will be acceptable before God. This same Hebrew word, *ratson*, is found in Exodus, where a turban with a gold plate engraved *Holy to the Lord* was placed on Aaron's

head. Here is what was said about this:

> *It shall regularly be on his forehead, that they may be accepted before the Lord.* **(Ex 28:38)**

Accepted in this passage is the same word, *ratson.*

A seal or sign upon the forehead which makes someone acceptable before God. What does that sound like? It sounds like the seal of God placed upon the 144,000 doesn't it? It is in this acceptable year that they and the great multitude of Rev 7:9-16 are raptured and spend a year of rest from their labors before God's Throne in heaven. They are made acceptable before Him.

To which some may say, "Come on, Isa 61:2 doesn't say anything about a rapture." Yes it does!

> *To proclaim the acceptable year of the Lord, and the day of vengeance of our God; to comfort all who mourn.* **(Isa 61:2)**

It's right there. Don't you see it? Most miss it.

Let's look at what Job says about those who mourn:

> *He sets on high those who are lowly, and those who mourn are lifted to safety.* **(Job 5:11)**

Lifted to safety? Yes. That is what the verse is all about. The acceptable year of the Lord is when the righteous are lifted to safety into the abode of the Lord. And our theory is that all of these things happen in the final year, the sabbatical year of Daniel's 70th Week.

But I'm sure you still have one question. Noah was in the ark —

Was the Flood a Picture of the Coming of the Wrath of God?

which is a picture of the safety of the rapture — for one year and ten days. But you may still be wondering about those *extra ten days*? After all, Hebraic years are all one year long, right? Well, all but one. The *year before a Jubilee is longer*; it is ten days longer to be exact. A year and ten days!

Hebraic secular years run from one *Rosh Hashanah* to another, in the same way that our years run from New Year's Day to New Year's Day. This is true for all secular Hebraic years — except the year before a Jubilee. That year runs from *Rosh Hashanah* to *Yom Kippur*. An extra ten days.

This is the exact length of time that Noah was in the ark. A traditional year, plus ten days. Our God is a God of absolute precision! The pictures He gave us in the accounts of the Old Testament are true and precise.

So, we have essentially proven our theory: That the account of the flood in Exodus, the three passages in Isaiah, and the fact that Daniel's 70th Week is an Hebraic shabua all point to Jesus returning at the Second Coming and pouring out his wrath *exactly* one year and ten days prior to the end of the seven years, contrary to everything we have been taught up to this point in time. Wow!

But you probably *still* have at least a couple of more questions. The one question nearly everyone asks is this: "I can understand that the un-righteous won't be able to live normal lives after the trumpet judgments begin, but what about the time during the seals and the Great Tribulation? Won't it be impossible to live a normal life even at that point?"

This will probably come as a shock to most, but the un-righteous will most likely live relatively normal lives during the Great

Tribulation. It's only the Christians and Jews that won't. Think about it. The Antichrist will control most of the world by the end of the Great Tribulation, so the wars that occurred earlier will cease. There will be plenty of food and little persecution for those who take the mark and worship the Beast. Only those Christians and Jews who refuse the mark will be persecuted unto death. It will be great tribulation for them, but not for the un-righteous.

The second question that nearly everyone asks is this: "I've read in scripture that no one can know the day or the hour of Jesus's return. This sure sounds like knowing the day and the hour — one year and ten days before the end is a pretty precise measurement of time."

That would be true if we had a perfect understanding of the way God tells time. The Hebraic calendar alternates between years with 353 or 354 days and those with 383 or 384 days. Plus there are those who believe that in the end times, all years will be exactly 360 days. So, there are at least five possible lengths of that final year. Do we really think our man-made calendars — even if they are based on the Bible — can match God's perfect understanding? I think not.

Finally, let's consider our verse about knowing the day and the hour:

> *But of that day and hour no one knows, not even the angels of heaven, nor the Son, but the Father alone.* **(Matt 24:36)**

The word *knows* in this verse is the Hebraic word *ido*, which means *to see with physical eyes and to know because you see*. So what this verse is saying, literally, is that only the Father knows,

Was the Flood a Picture of the Coming of the Wrath of God?

because He *sees*.

Some believe Jesus may return on the new moon of a future *Rosh Hashanah*. Even if this is true, perhaps the thick clouds, the dark, and the gloom that the Bible predicts for the end times will prevent everyone from seeing the moon, thereby precluding them from knowing that this is *the* day. In that case, *only* the Father will know. This is an understanding that is not commonly taught. With God, all things are possible.

Article Thirteen

When is The Day of the Lord?

The *Day of the Lord* is possibly the most frequently addressed end times topic in the Bible, with nearly three dozen total references. Considering most scholars agree that it's synonymous with the wrath of God and that the rapture occurs just prior to this day, discovering the timing of this particular day should also uncover the timing of the rapture. We have four aspects of the Day of the Lord to discover:

1. How many Days of the Lord are there?

2. How long is The Day of the Lord?

3. What happens on that day?

4. When does it take place in the chronology of the end times?

The phrase, *Day of the Lord* refers primarily to a time period when God alone is exalted and the arrogance of man is ended. In this way, the Day of the Lord is contrasted with the day we are currently living in the *day of man*. It will be a time period when God vindicates Himself and pours out wrath on Israel and the Gentile nations in punishment for their rejection of Him.

We call this the eschatological Day of the Lord in the Old Testament. Other, more minor, periods of God's judgment on Israel are also occasionally called Days of the Lord, so it is important to differentiate in the Old Testament passages which are being referred to.

When is the Day of the Lord?

The *initiation* of the final eschatological Day of the Lord is, of course, a single day. The *phrase*, Day of the Lord, may actually include a longer period of time. For example, the Pre-Tribulation rapture theory considers the entire seven-year Tribulation to be the Day of the Lord. And some scholars consider that the entire thousand year Millennial Kingdom is the Day of the Lord. Most of these are assumptions.

As we discussed in the previous article, Isaiah contains three specific indications that the Day of the Lord's wrath starts on a day and is also one year in length, such as Isaiah 34:8, Isaiah 63:4, and the famous passage at Isaiah 61:2, which was quoted by Jesus:

> *For the Lord has a day of vengeance, A year of recompense for the cause of Zion.* **(Isa 34:8)**

> *For the day of vengeance was in My heart, And My year of redemption has come.* **(Isa 63:4)**

> *To proclaim the favorable year of the Lord and the day of vengeance of our God; To comfort all who mourn.* **(Isa 61:2)**

From these three verses, we also find the principal purposes of the time of God's wrath. It is a time of recompense, or punishment, of the wicked. It is a time when Jesus will bring redemption to the unsaved of Israel. And it is a favorable time for Christians, who will be raptured into the presence of God. The Day of the Lord encompasses all three of these purposes.

The prophet Zephaniah summarizes other factors about the final eschatological Day of the Lord, as well. It is a day of wrath, distress, destruction, and darkness:

> *Near is the great day of the Lord, Near and coming very quickly; Listen, the day of the Lord! In it the warrior cries out bitterly. A day of wrath is that day, A day of trouble and distress, A day of destruction and desolation, A day of darkness and gloom, A day of clouds and thick darkness.* **(Zeph 1:14-15)**

Let's look at passages which indicate when the Day of the Lord begins. In fact, let's build a timeline displaying all of the precursors of the Day of the Lord.

Earlier, we learned that the Day of the Lord will not come *unless* the *apostasy and revealing* of Antichrist occurs *first*, after the midpoint of the Tribulation, as reported in 2 Thess:

> *Don't let anyone deceive you in any way, for that day will not come until the rebellion occurs and the man of lawlessness is revealed, the man doomed to destruction. He will oppose and will exalt himself over everything that is called God or is worshiped, so that he sets himself up in God's temple, proclaiming himself to be God.* **(2 Thess 2:3-4)**

This precursor eliminates the entire first half of the Tribulation as a possibility for the beginning of the Day of the Lord. Figure 13-1 is a depiction of what this looks like:

When is the Day of the Lord?

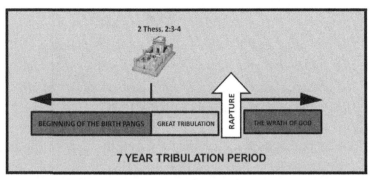

Figure 13-1

Now, we will build on this timeline after we have investigated a number of other scriptures which help us establish the timing of the rapture. Isaiah provides the first of these important scripture passages:

> *The proud look of man will be abased and the loftiness of man will be humbled, and the Lord alone will be exalted in that day.* **(Isa 2:11-12)**

Only God is exalted on the Day of the Lord. This precludes the Antichrist from being exalted on that day, and it precludes the Day the Lord and the Great Tribulation from being simultaneous — obviously, the Antichrist is exalted during the Great Tribulation, so they can't happen at the same time. So let's add Isa 2 to our list of precursors.

We also learned previously that the wrath of God begins after the *time marker* verse of Rev 6:17:

> *For the great day of their wrath has come, and who is able to stand?* **(Rev 6:17)**

Notice it says the *great day*. This is the Day of the Lord, so we can add the time marker verse of Rev 6:17 to our timeline. It marks the beginning of the day when the Day of the Lord's wrath will finally be poured out. The time marker verse occurs right after the sixth seal, which is the darkening of the sun, moon, and stars.

There are a number of verses that reference both the Day of the Lord and this darkening. Isa 13 refers to the darkening of the sun, moon, and stars on the Day of the Lord:

> *For the stars of heaven and their constellations will not flash forth their light; the sun will be dark when it rises and the moon will not shed its light.* **(Isa 13:10)**

Joel 3 tells us the Day of the Lord is near when the *sixth seal* sign occurs:

> *Multitudes, multitudes in the valley of decision! For the day of the Lord is near in the valley of decision. The sun and moon grow dark and the stars lose their brightness.* **(Joel 3:14-15)**

Notice that it is *near*; it hasn't happened yet. And Joel 2 informs us that these six seal signs happen *before* the Day of the Lord:

> *The sun will be turned into darkness and the moon into blood before the great and awesome day of the Lord comes.* **(Joel 2:31)**

Notice also that it is the *great day*, just as our time marker verse tells us. So, we can add the sixth seal and it's sign of the *darkening* of the sun, moon, and stars to our timeline. This is the event that cuts short the Great Tribulation, per Matt 24:22. So that is where we are adding it on our timeline.

When is the Day of the Lord?

Silence before the Lord in heaven is another sign that must take place before the Day of the Lord's wrath. We find this reference in Zeph 1:

> *Be silent before the Lord God! For the day of the Lord is near, for the Lord has prepared a sacrifice, He has consecrated His guests.* **(Zeph 1:7)**

The sacrifice the Lord has prepared is the fiery judgment He is about to pour out on the un-repentant. And who are His guests in heaven? Why the raptured Christians, of course! When does this take place? There is only *one time* recorded in the Bible when *praise stops* in heaven. Amazingly, this happens upon the breaking of the *seventh seal*, further pin-pointing the timing of the Day of a Lord's wrath:

> *When the Lamb broke the seventh seal, there was silence in heaven for about half an hour.* **(Rev 8:1)**

So we will add silence before the Lord in heaven and the seventh seal, which take place after the rapture, but before the Lord's wrath.

We now have a completed timeline, with all of our important scripture references included:

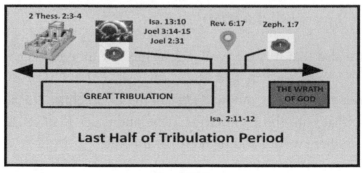

Figure 13-2

In addition to this amazing timeline — which totally precludes the Day of the Lord from occurring at the beginning of the Tribulation — God has given us two more time markers for this time period. First, Elijah will return prior to the coming of the Lord's wrath:

> *Behold, I am going to send you Elijah the prophet before the coming of the great and terrible day of the Lord.* **(Mal 4:5)**

Many believe Elijah may be one of the two witnesses of Rev 11. But because we are unsure of the timing of their ministry and Elijah's identity, let's not add this passage to the timeline. However, it seems to support our thesis, as well.

Second, from Paul we also see that the Day of the Lord's wrath and destruction will come upon the un-repentant at the moment they are saying "peace and safety:"

> *For you yourselves know full well that the day of the Lord will come just like a thief in the night. While they are saying, "Peace and safety!" then destruction will come upon them suddenly like labor pains upon a woman with child, and they will not escape.* **(1 Thess. 5:2-3)**

When is this? There are two possibilities. If you remember, we have shown that the Great Tribulation ends for the elect upon the sixth seal and it's signs of the darkening of the sun and moon and falling of the stars. The un-repentant, unsaved Jews will have been persecuted severely up until this point. Perhaps it's at this point, when the persecution seems to have ended, that they will say, "Finally, peace and safety." And while they are

When is the Day of the Lord?

saying this, Jesus appears in the sky, and then the wrath of God is poured out.

It is also possible that the Gentile nations will say this a few days prior to the sixth seal being opened. If this is the moment, the two witnesses are killed by the beast, then the great celebration that the world holds for this event may happen.

We just don't know for sure. Paul doesn't give us quite enough information for us to place this precursor on our timeline. However, even without these last two precursors, the timeline is overwhelming evidence that the Day of the Lord's wrath begins *after the sixth seal*. And this is *highly problematic* for Pre-Tribulation supporters.

Paul had these additional things to say about the Day of the Lord in 1 Cor:

> *So that you are not lacking in any gift, awaiting eagerly the revelation of our Lord Jesus Christ, who will also confirm you to the end, blameless in the day of our Lord Jesus Christ.* **(1 Cor 1:7-8)**

Paul said that Christians will be sustained until the Day of the Lord and that Jesus's blood will enable us to be found guiltless on that day. Paul also indicated that a man's spirit is saved upon the Day of the Lord, again indicating that the rapture happens on that day:

> *I have decided to deliver such a one to Satan for the destruction of his flesh, so that his spirit may be saved in the day of the Lord Jesus.* **(1 Cor 5:5)**

So what do Pre-Tribulation proponents have to say about these things? Initially, Pre-Tribulation rapture scholars like Cooper,

Walvoord, and Hodges realized that scripture clearly teaches the Day of the Lord follows the rapture. They assumed the entire seven-year Tribulation was the Day of the Lord. However, when Marvin Rosenthal's *Pre-Wrath Rapture of the Church* was written in the early 1990s, it brought to light all these precursors, which disproved the popular Pre-Tribulation position.

In response, Pre-Tribulation followers have said that there were *two* Days of the Lord — an intense, or narrow, one that started after the sixth seal, and a less-intense, or broad, one that started right after their supposed Pre-Tribulation rapture. Rather than admitting that they may have been wrong about the timing of the rapture, they appear to have just made something up.

Of course, that is not what the scriptures teach. The term Day of the Lord is a specific, technical term. As we've seen in all of the examples in this article, there is one and *only one* eschatological Day of the Lord's wrath that is coming. God alone will be exalted on that day. And all of the time markers we have identified clearly point to a period that begins *after* the sixth seal, which completely eliminates the Pre-Tribulation rapture theory as a possibility.

Article Fourteen

Taken or Left?

As we have learned from our earlier discussions of the term *rapture*, there will be a great separation of the righteous from the un-righteous when Jesus comes again. Unfortunately, like so many other facets of the rapture debate, Christians can't decide which people are likely to be *taken* and which may be *left* behind.

> *Then there will be two men in the field; one will be taken and one will be left* (**Matt 24:40**)

In fact, this disagreement has become so divisive that even if we push the Pre-Tribulation discussion aside for the moment, Christians can't seem to agree whether it's the *righteous* that are taken in the rapture or the *un-righteous* that are snatched away for judgment.

> *Then there will be two men in the field; one will be taken and one will be left. Two women will be grinding at the mill; one will be taken and one will be left. Therefore be on the alert, for you do not know which day your Lord is coming. But be sure of this, that if the head of the house had known at what time of the night the thief was coming, he would have been on the alert and would not have allowed his house to be broken into.* (**Matt 24:40-43**)

If you read the scripture plainly, this discussion about being taken or left is an attempt to further define the subject that Jesus was speaking about in the various other verses of Matt 24. In these verses we have already learned that Matt 24:31 is the rapture and not the Second Coming, so this is an application of the rapture. And, obviously, if it is an application of the rapture, then it is the righteous that are taken.

Jesus further reinforces this idea through his parable of the thief in the night, as a way of admonishing believers to be ready for His return — although we have already demonstrated that the return of Jesus will be no surprise, coming as it does precisely 1,260 days following the *abomination of desolation*. The Greek words used in this passage also help us to clearly understand who is taken and who is left. The Greek word *paralambono*, meaning *taken*, is found in this famous rapture passage in John 14:

> *In My Father's house are many dwelling places; if it were not so, I would have told you; for I go to prepare a place for you. If I go and prepare a place for you, I will come again and receive you to Myself, that where I am, there you may be also.* **(John 14:2-3)**

Obviously this is a picture of the rapture, because the righteous are taken. Who else would Jesus be preparing a place for?

This same Greek word, *paralambono*, is used in a *marriage* context in Matt 1:

> *And Joseph awoke from his sleep and did as the angel of the Lord commanded him, and took Mary as his wife, but kept her a virgin until she gave birth to a Son; and he called His name Jesus.* **(Matt 1:24-25)**

Here we see that Joseph took Mary to be his wife. This is an intimate taking, not a taking in the context of judgment. But when Jesus confronted the Pharisees and pronounced judgment on them in Matt 23, He used the word *left*. The Greek word *aphiemi* — those who'll be left are those who will be *judged*.

> *Behold, your house is being left to you desolate!* **(Matt 23:38)**

This same Greek word — *aphiemi* — also means *divorce*.

> *But to the rest I say, not the Lord, that if any brother has a wife who is an unbeliever, and she consents to live with him, he must not divorce her* **(1 Cor 7:12)**

It is very clear from the Greek words found in these passages exactly who will be taken and who will be left: The righteous are taken, and the un-righteous are divorced.

Despite the strong evidence found within scripture and supported by the more original Greek translations, some Christians look to the parable of the wheat and the tares as evidence that *both* the wheat and the weeds are gathered. In fact, when Jesus is later explaining the parable, He says the *weeds are gathered out* of his Kingdom.

> *Allow both to grow together until the harvest; and in the time of the harvest I will say to the reapers, "First gather up the tares and bind them in bundles to burn them up; but gather the wheat into my barn.* **(Matt 13:30)**

Jesus uses two words for gather in this passage, and they are different words in the Greek, with different meanings. We saw earlier that Jesus used the word *sunago* for the *gathering* of the wheat, and derivatives of this word are used for the rapture in Matt 24:31, Mark 13:27, and 2 Thess 2:1.

Taken or Left?

Additionally, whereas the gathering of weeds uses *sullego*, which is a spoken gathering, as in *Jesus will speak judgment* upon the un-righteous, *sunago* is an assisted gathering, performed by the angels.

In *every* biblical example that Jesus gave us of the separation of the righteous from the un-righteous, it is the righteous who are taken.

- Noah and his family were *taken* above the flood in the ark, while the un-righteous were left to drown.

- Lot and his family were *taken* to safety by angels, while Sodom and the cities of the plain were left to burn in judgment.

- In the parable of the ten virgins, the five wise virgins were *taken* into the wedding feast, while the five foolish virgins were left behind to suffer judgment.

- And in the most important example of all, in the rapture depicted in Matt 24:31, it is the elect Christians who are *taken* to be with Jesus.

There is absolutely no question from Matt 24:31 who are taken and who are left. The only reason this event is even remotely controversial is because some Christians confuse the coming of Jesus at this event with the Second Coming. But let's be clear. This is the rapture. It is *not* the Second Coming.

As we see yet again, in Noah's flood it was the *un-righteous* who were *swept away*:

> *For as in those days before the flood they were eating and drinking, marrying and giving in marriage, until the day that Noah entered the ark, and they did not understand until the flood came and took them all away; so will the coming of the Son of Man be.* **(Matt 24:38-39)**

Unfortunately, some translations of the Greek word which lies behind this translation substituted the English word *took* — as in took them away. Because this was a form of the English word *take*, readers thought it was the un-righteous that were taken. But, we clearly see that the two Greek verbs found in these verses are completely different ideas. There is *no* substantiation for the idea that the un-righteous are taken in this passage.

The passage about who is taken and who is left in Matt 24:40-41 is an application of what preceded it, and that is the gathering of the elect in Matt 24:31 and the coming of Jesus, as in the days of Noah. Because we have now proven it is the righteous that are taken in these events, these events *must* refer to the rapture and resurrection.

But as a final attempt to disprove this understanding, some scholars will look at Luke 17 for evidence that it is the wicked that are taken. After Jesus gave a long teaching on both Noah and Lot being taken to safety, He summarized His teaching by saying that *one will be taken and one will be left*. To which the disciples asked, "Where, Lord?"

> *Two men will be in the field; one will be taken and the other will be left." And answering they said to Him, "Where, Lord?"* **(Luke 17:36-37)**

Taken or Left?

Now, this question is incomplete. It can mean one of two things: Either the disciples were asking. "Where does this happen, Lord?" or they were asking, "Where are they taken, Lord?" Either meaning is possible. Those who prefer to think taken is *taken to judgment* look at Jesus's answer and say, "Aha, they are taken to be killed, and the eagles [vultures] eat their corpses."

> *"Where the body is, there also the vultures will be gathered."* **(Luke 17:37)**

But this ignores all of Jesus's previous teaching in Luke 17. Jesus taught that Noah was taken to *safety*. He taught that Lot was taken to *safety*. Even Lot's wife was being taken to *safety* — until she looked back and was turned to a pillar of salt.

And finally, in Luke 17:31, Jesus instructs the righteous not to waste time getting their belongings. This only makes sense if they are the ones taken. It they are left, they have all the time in the world to get their belongings.

All of these passages and examples illustrate that it is the *righteous* who are taken to safety. So that means that the disciples were asking the first question, "Where does this happen," as opposed to the second question, "Where are they taken?" I'm sure this is a surprise to most of you. If that is so, and the disciples were asking the first question, then what does this cryptic phrase about *eagles* mean?

First, notice that *body* is singular. If this verse were talking about the taking of the un-righteous to judgment, then it would be plural: Where the *bodies* are. But that's not what it says. It says *body*, as in *body of Christ*. The Greek word here is *soma*, *which* can be a living body, or a dead body.

Second, notice that it is *eagles* that are gathered together. The Greek word used here is *not* the word for *vultures*. And this passage might not be talking about birds at all. In the Bible angelic and heavenly beings are depicted as eagles, or like eagles. For instance, 10 times in Revelation the cherubim have one face like an eagle. And in Rev 8:13, an eagle messenger — that is almost certainly an angel — announces the eternal Gospel to the world. Might this verse in Luke be referring to angels, as well?

Why exactly did the disciples ask the question, "Where, Lord?" Because they were interested in knowing where the gathering or taking of the righteous will happen. Jesus's answer, then, was logical. *Where the body is* — the body of Christ — there the angels will be gathered together. Wherever a Christian is dead or alive, there will be the angel gatherers. Think about it!

This passage about eagles is a very difficult passage to understand, and the concept regarding who is taken and who is left is difficult, as well. That is why there has been so much controversy for so many years. But if we carefully examine scripture, we find that it is entirely consistent and supports the taking of the righteous to heaven in a Pre-Wrath rapture.

Article Fifteen

What is the Order of Seals, Trumpets, and Bowls?

The book of Revelation sets forth the chronology of the end times in amazing detail in the form of three sets of sevens: Seven seals, seven trumpets, and seven bowls. There is only one problem. Most Christians can't agree on the order of these events. If you read scripture plainly, the seven seals come first, in Rev 6:1-8:5. Next, the seven trumpets are blown in order in Rev 8:6-11:19. Then, finally, the seven bowls are poured out in Rev 15:7-16:17. So the plain reading of scripture is that the seals all come first, then all the trumpets, and then all the bowls, with no overlap. Here is what that looks like:

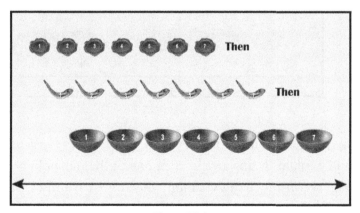

Figure 15-1

But those who hold to a Post-Tribulation rapture theory, and even some of those who support the Pre-Tribulation theory, have trouble with that plain reading. Because this places the *time marker* verse of Rev 6:17 — which indicates that the wrath of God has begun — long before the end of the tribulation. And it also places the seventh trumpet — which many associate with the Second Coming — before the end, as well.

Although the Pre-Wrath rapture theory is completely consistent with the plain reading of scripture, many who hold to these other theories have attempted to construct other chronologies to better support their views. For instance, one of these views is that all the *firsts* occur first: First seal, first trumpet, and first bowl. This is followed by all of the *seconds*, then all of the *thirds* — and on until all of the *sevenths* happen at the same time. That process would look something like this:

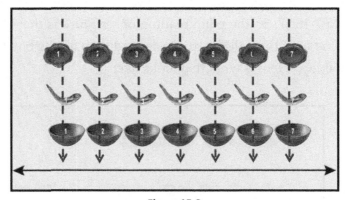

Figure 15-2

There are numerous problems with this theory, most of which we will explain in this article. But one of the most obvious ones is that, according to Revelation, the fourth trumpet dims the light of the sun by two thirds, while the fourth Bowl intensifies it, so that those on earth can be scorched. Obviously, both of these cannot occur at the same time.

There are dozens of other, random orders which have been proposed for the seals, trumpets, and bowls. However, despite whatever randomness exists in these other sequences, nearly all of the proposed chronologies feature the sixth seal near the end, and a concurrent seventh seal, trumpet, and bowl at the end, as well. This is due to a misunderstanding that Matt 24 and Rev 19 represent the same event: The Second Coming. We previously learned that they are *not* the same events. Matt 24 is the rapture, while Rev 19 is the Second Coming.

So although it's the plain reading of scripture that all the seals come before all the trumpets, which come before all the bowls, can we find other proof in Revelation that support this plain reading that the seals, trumpets, and bowls occur in the order in which they are found in scripture! The answer is *yes*! There is overwhelming additional evidence. That evidence is found at the point the seals end and the trumpets begin, and again at the point where the trumpets end and the bowls begin.

The first piece of evidence is that there are similar, but not exact, *transition events* that occur between each major set of events, such as the seals, trumpets, and bowls. And these transition events make clear that the events that follow them are distinct and do not overlap. Let's look at these transitions.

Before the seals, there is a thundering and a lightning event. Before the trumpets, there is an earthquake, which is added to the thundering and lightning. Before the bowls, there is a hailstorm, which is added to the thundering, lightning, and earthquake. And, finally, before the Second Coming, we are told the hailstones weigh a hundred pounds and the earthquake is the most severe in history.

There is an obvious *difference* and *worsening* in each of these transition events. If you read the text of Revelation in Greek, it is obvious that all the seals come before all the trumpets. The text uses the special *aorist* tense, which is the tense the Bible

What Is the Order of Seals, Trumpets and Bowls?

traditionally uses to tell a continuous narrative. And the phrases in this ongoing narrative are separated by *kai*, which means *and* or *then*, again showing a continuous narrative.

Reinforcing this is the proof found in Rev 7:2-3, where we see that the angels are specifically instructed not to harm the trees, earth, or sea until after the 144,000 are sealed:

> *And I saw another angel ascending from the rising of the sun, having the seal of the living God; and he cried out with a loud voice to the four angels to whom it was granted to harm the earth and the sea, saying, "Do not harm the earth or the sea or the trees until we have sealed the bond-servants of our God on their foreheads."* **(Rev 7:2-3)**

Yet the first three trumpets harmed these exact things. Obviously, the sixth seal must come before even the first trumpet is blown. The very language of the text precludes anything but a sequential order. First the seventh seal is broken. Then — and only then — are the trumpets given to the angels:

> *When the Lamb broke the seventh seal, there was silence in heaven for about half an hour. And I saw the seven angels who stand before God, and seven trumpets were given to them.* **(Rev 8:1-2)**

If the transition between the seals and trumpets seems to preclude anything but a sequential order, the one between the trumpets and bowls may be even stronger proof of that sequential order. Let's look at the order of these events. In Rev 11 we learn first that the seventh trumpet is blown:

> *Then the seventh angel sounded; and there were loud voices in heaven, saying, "The kingdom of the world has*

become the kingdom of our Lord and of His Christ; and He will reign forever and ever." **(Rev 11:15)**

Then, after the trumpet, the Temple in heaven is opened:

And the temple of God which is in heaven was opened; and the ark of His covenant appeared in His temple, and there were flashes of lightning and sounds and peals of thunder and an earthquake and a great hailstorm. **(Rev 11:19)**

Later, in later in Rev 15, we see this same time marking event — the opening of the Temple:

After these things I looked, and the temple of the tabernacle of testimony in heaven was opened. **(Rev 15:5)**

Only *after* that are the angels given the bowls of wrath. This precludes the bowls from occurring during the trumpets. They *must* come after.

Let's examine this order of events one more time, because it's profound. In Rev 11, the seventh trumpet is blown, and after that the Temple in heaven is opened. In both Rev 11 and Rev 15, only *after* that are the bowls of wrath distributed to the angels. Under no circumstance can the trumpets and bowls be concurrent events. All the trumpets are blown before a single bowl is poured out.

From all of this evidence, it seems overwhelmingly clear that the seals, trumpets, and bowls occur consecutively, in the order they are found in scripture: All the seals come before all the trumpets, which then come before all the bowls.

Article Sixteen

The Resurrection and Rapture Timing

We know from the most significant rapture passage in the Bible — 1 Thess 4:15-17 — that a resurrection of all the dead in Christ precedes the rapture:

> *For the Lord Himself will descend from heaven with a shout, with the voice of the archangel and with the trumpet of God, and the dead in Christ will rise first. Then we who are alive and remain will be caught up together with them in the clouds to meet the Lord in the air, and so we shall always be with the Lord.* **(1 Thess 4:16-17)**

This suggests that if we are able to ascertain the timing of this resurrection, we can then determine the timing of the rapture. Of course, we have already proven that this passage from 1 Thess 4 is the same event as Matt 24:29-31, but not the same event as Rev 19:11-15. We therefore know in advance that this resurrection happens after the sixth seal, and after the Great Tribulation.

Now, scholars are widely divided on how many resurrections there will be. Some say three; some say as many as seven. So our first task is to determine how many resurrections will occur. Luckily there is a scriptural passage which directly provides this information:

> *For as in Adam all die, so also in Christ all will be made alive. But each in his own order: Christ the first fruits, after that those who are Christ's at His*

The Resurrection and Rapture Timing

> *coming, then comes the end, when He hands over the kingdom to the God and Father, when He has abolished all rule and all authority and power. For He must reign until He has put all His enemies under His feet. The last enemy that will be abolished is death.* **(1 Cor 15:22-26)**

This passage specifically gives us the order of resurrections. And as we shall see, there are three — and *only three* — resurrections: One in the first century, when Jesus was raised from the dead; one at the inception or beginning of Jesus's coming, or *parousia;* and then one at the end. But the end of what?

It is the end or completion of the Thousand Year Reign of Christ. We know that because it is only at this point that Jesus abolishes death and throws it into the lake of fire, per Rev 20:14. Paul has given us an abundantly clear passage. There are three, and *only* three, resurrections. This makes perfect sense, because Paul uses the term *firstfruits* to describe Jesus's resurrection, the first resurrection.

Firstfruits is a harvest term, and Paul is comparing the three resurrections to a Jewish harvest. The three parts of a Jewish harvest were the *firstfruits*, the *main harvest*, and then the *gleanings harvest*. During the firstfruits portion, the first ripe grain was harvested and waved before the Lord as an offering. This was a promise of the coming future harvest. The resurrection of Jesus performed this role back in the first century.

The *main harvest* takes place when the majority of the grain is harvested. This is the resurrection that will take place at the inception of Jesus's coming, or *parousia*. We know that this takes place in 1 Thess 4 15-17, and it is also pictured in Matt 24:30-31, when the newly resurrected and those still surviving the Great Tribulation are *gathered together*, which is yet another harvest term.

Finally, a *gleanings harvest* takes place at the end to ensure that no grain is left behind. The resurrection at the end of the Millennial Kingdom will accomplish this purpose.

Let's construct a timeline of resurrections. Initially there is a firstfruits, then the main harvest resurrection at the inception or coming of Jesus, which will happen immediately before the rapture. And, finally, a gleanings harvest will happen at the end of the Millennial Kingdom:

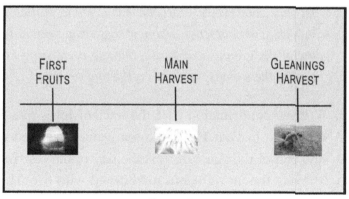

Figure 16-1

Now that we have this timeline constructed, let's place the Bible's resurrection passages on it to see where they fall.

1. **Matt 27:52-53**: We see that after Jesus's resurrection many Old Testament saints were resurrected, as well. We can place this passage with the firstfruits resurrection.

The Resurrection and Rapture Timing

> *The tombs were opened, and many bodies of the saints who had fallen asleep were raised; and coming out of the tombs after His resurrection they entered the holy city and appeared to many.*

2. In **Dan 12:1-2** we see a resurrection of Daniel's people after the Great Tribulation. Thus, all Jewish saints who placed their faith in Messiah even before He was born will be raised during the main harvest, after the Great Tribulation.

> *Now at that time Michael, the great prince who stands guard over the sons of your people, will arise. And there will be a time of distress such as never occurred since there was a nation until that time; and at that time your people, everyone who is found written in the book, will be rescued. Many of those who sleep in the dust of the ground will awake, these to everlasting life, but the others to disgrace and everlasting contempt.*

3. We see confirmation that the ancient Jews rise at this time in **Dan 12:13**. We see Daniel is raised at the end of the age, which is the day of harvest and the day the un-righteous are burned with fire. This passage says that everyone written in the Book of Life will be raised at this same time.

> *But as for you, go your way to the end; then you will enter into rest and rise again for your allotted portion at the end of the age."*

4. The resurrection will take place in the context of **Matt 24:30-31**, which is at the coming, or *parousia*,

of Jesus. So we can add Matt 24 to our timeline, as well.

And then the sign of the Son of Man will appear in the sky, and then all the tribes of the earth will mourn, and they will see the Son of Man coming on the clouds of the sky with power and great glory. And He will send forth His angels with a great trumpet and they will gather together His elect from the four winds, from one end of the sky to the other.

5. And **1 Thess 4:15-17** must fall here, as well. Not only have we already proven that Matt 24:30-31 is the same passage as we have in 1 Thess 4, but according to Paul there are *only* three resurrections. There is no room for extra resurrections, like before the Tribulation Period.

For this we say to you by the word of the Lord, that we who are alive and remain until the coming of the Lord, will not precede those who have fallen asleep. For the Lord Himself will descend from heaven with a shout, with the voice of the archangel and with the trumpet of God, and the dead in Christ will rise first. Then we who are alive and remain will be caught up together with them in the clouds to meet the Lord in the air, and so we shall always be with the Lord.

6. We see the final *gleanings* resurrection that happens after Jesus's one-thousand-year Millennial Reign in **Rev 20:12-13**. We can also place this passage on the timeline. This is a gleanings because the only righteous who are resurrected at this time are those who died after the rapture, a much smaller number

The Resurrection and Rapture Timing

than the vast multitudes resurrected at the main harvest. In addition to this limited number of righteous who will be resurrected, all of the unrighteous dead from all the ages are resurrected at this time.

And I saw the dead, the great and the small, standing before the throne, and books were opened; and another book was opened, which is the book of life; and the dead were judged from the things which were written in the books, according to their deeds. And the sea gave up the dead which were in it, and death and Hades gave up the dead which were in them; and they were judged, every one of them according to their deeds.

So here is what our timeline looks like with all of the applicable scriptures applied:

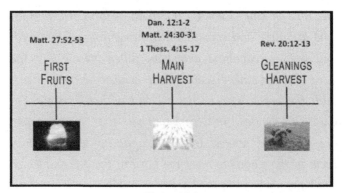

Figure 16-2

In addition to the passages that we just looked at that are rather easy to ascertain, there are also some difficult passages to consider, like John 11:24:

Martha said to Him, "I know that he will rise again in the resurrection on the last day." **(John 11:24)**

Post-Tribulation believers will say, "See, the resurrection is on the last day of the tribulation." But that is not what the passage says. It simply says *the last day*. But the last day of what?

The last day of this age is the most likely answer. We have already seen that Daniel will be raised at the end of the age. And we have learned that the end of the age is when the harvest takes place. However, nowhere have we read that the end of the age is the end of the Tribulation period. The end of the age is dependent on the timing of the rapture, and we have established that this comes after the sixth seal and before all the trumpet and bowl judgments

Another difficult passage is Rev 20:4-5.

> *Then I saw thrones, and they sat on them, and judgment was given to them. And I saw the souls of those who had been beheaded because of their testimony of Jesus and because of the word of God, and those who had not worshiped the beast or his image, and had not received the mark on their forehead and on their hand; and they came to life and reigned with Christ for a thousand years. The rest of the dead did not come to life until the thousand years were completed. This is the first resurrection.* **(Rev 20:4-5)**

Pre-Tribulation proponents say this is a separate, extra resurrection of those who died during the Tribulation. Post-Tribulation followers say it is the main harvest resurrection that happens after Armageddon. However, neither is correct.

The Resurrection and Rapture Timing

If we refer back to the beginnings of our timeline again, we recall from 1 Cor 15 that there are three, and only three, resurrections. In combination with what we just learned from Rev 20, the main harvest resurrection, the first resurrection, includes those martyred by the Beast. This seems to preclude a Pre-Tribulation rapture theory.

In response, Pre-Tribulation rapture theorists contend that the resurrection scene in Rev 20 is the *first of its kind, not the first in time*. This phrase means that the first resurrection is, in their minds, the resurrection of the righteous, and that there can be multiple resurrections of the righteous. Thus, the resurrection that happens in Rev 20 is simply the resurrection of those who are martyred during the Tribulation period. It is also the second main harvest resurrection, the second resurrection of the righteous.

This makes some sense, until we return to the passage in 1 Cor 15 where we see that the main harvest resurrection, or the first resurrection, occurs at Jesus's coming. This phrase, *at his coming*, is found multiple times in the New Testament and *always* refers to the very beginning, or inception, of that coming, or *parousia*. It *never* refers to events that occur during a longer event. This totally precludes there being multiple first resurrections.

And since we know that the first resurrection includes those martyred by the Beast, it means that the first resurrection happens *after* the Great Tribulation and *precludes* a Pre-Tribulation rapture.

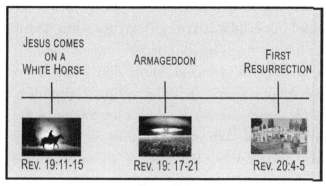

Figure 16-3

Now let's look at what those who support the Post-Tribulation rapture theory think of this difficult message. Referring once again to our timeline, we see that the position of the passage in Revelation comes *after* Jesus comes on a white horse, and *after* He lands on earth and fights the Battle of Armageddon. Yet, 1 Thess 4 tells us that the first resurrection, the main harvest resurrection, happens while Jesus is still in the air. From this we can determine that this passage in Revelation is *not* in chronological order. That's what makes it an extremely difficult passage to properly time.

However, John gives us a clue about when it happens. The clue regards *who* is included in the resurrection: The *souls of the martyrs* of the fifth seal. Look at the comparisons between the passages in Rev 6 and Rev 20. They are both called souls. They both died for their testimony and the Word of God. And if the fifth seal martyrs are included, it places this passage back at the time we have determined the return of Jesus takes place, after the sixth seal, not at the end, as the position of this passage seems to indicate.

The Resurrection and Rapture Timing

So why is the resurrection reference made at the end of Revelation and out of place? We can't say for sure. But it appears that John is stressing the concept of the thousand-year reign of these resurrected saints and Jesus. John mentions this reign six separate times in this chapter. It is the focus of the entire chapter. So it isn't the timing of the resurrection within the 70th week of Daniel *per se* that this verse details, but, rather, the fate of those who are resurrected. Additionally, it allows John to demonstrate that there are two resurrections — one on each side of this thousand-year reign.

In conclusion, 1 Cor 15:22-26 is the *key verse* for determining the number and order of resurrections. There are three, and only three, resurrections. And the main harvest resurrection that takes place immediately before the rapture takes place at the inception or beginning of the *parousia*, or coming, of Jesus, which we now know occurs in Matt 24:32 31, after the Great Tribulation and after the sixth seal. This completely eliminates the possibility of a Pre-Tribulation rapture.

Article Seventeen

The Great Multitude

We have previously demonstrated that the rapture occurs after the sixth seal and that the raptured saints appear before the Throne of God in heaven immediately after that rapture. Because the saints in this multitude of Rev 7:9 are *said* to have come out of the Great Tribulation, this *disproves* the Pre-Tribulation rapture theory and supports the Pre-Wrath theory. Therefore, if we are able to *prove* that these are raptured saints that came out of the Great Tribulation, not only will we have disproven the Pre-Tribulation rapture, but we will have disproven the Mid-Tribulation and Post-Tribulation rapture theories, as well. None of these theories believe that the saints are raptured between the 6th and 7th seals.

So let's look at some of the differences between souls that come out of the Great Tribulation and the raptured saints who are in resurrection bodies.

1. Souls might be identified as such, while those in bodies might not be.

2. Souls would be disembodied, while those in resurrection bodies would by definition have bodies.

3. Souls would arrive one by one as they died, while raptured saints would arrive *en masse*.

4. Jesus informs us that the souls of the righteous dead are in a holding place that He termed

Abraham's bosom in the book of Luke, while it is likely resurrected saints would be free to stand before the Throne of God.

Fortunately, scripture provides us with a definitive look at souls in heaven prior to being resurrected and raptured. This allows us to compare these souls with the great multitude of Rev 7:9.

When Jesus opens the fifth seal, we are told that the souls of martyrs from all the ages cry out:

> *When the Lamb broke the fifth seal, I saw underneath the altar the souls of those who had been slain because of the word of God, and because of the testimony which they had maintained ... And there was given to each of them a white robe; and they were told that they should rest for a little while longer, until the number of their fellow servants and their brethren who were to be killed even as they had been, would be completed also.* **(Rev 6:9, 11)**

Let's see how this passage compares with the traits of souls we just described.

1. They are specifically called souls, not saints or bondservants.

2. They are kept in a special holding area — in this case, it is described as being under the altar in heaven.

3. We learn their number is incomplete, that there will be more added to this number prior to the rapture.

4. We see that they are given a white robe; but we don't see them putting the robe on. Why is that? It's because they are disembodied. They don't have a body to put the robe on yet. They have not been given a resurrection body.

So the saints beneath the altar represent the baseline of what souls in heaven are like. So let's re-examine our list of the traits of souls and compare it to the souls of the fifth seal martyrs:

1. They are certainly called souls.

2. They are disembodied, because they aren't seen wearing their robes.

3. They certainly arrive in heaven one at a time.

4. They are in a special holding area under the altar.

If we were to see changes to this baseline state when we examine the great multitude, then we might believe they were no longer souls, but, rather, saints in resurrection bodies.

Changes is an understatement! Everything has changed!

> *After these things I looked, and behold, a great multitude which no one could count, from every nation and all tribes and peoples and tongues, standing before the throne and before the Lamb, clothed in white robes, and palm branches were in their hands.* **(Rev 7:9)**

Here's what's changed:

1. They are no longer called souls.

2. Their location has changed: They are no longer under the altar in a holding area, but now stand before the Throne of God.

3. Their number isn't being added to; rather, they seem to have appeared all at once. John is surprised to see them and says, "I looked and behold a great multitude."

4. They now have bodies — resurrection bodies. And they are able to wear their white robes.

5. As if to emphasize the point that they now have bodies, John points out that they are *standing* on their feet and holding palm branches in their hands.

So let's re-examine our list of the traits of those with resurrection bodies and compare it to the great multitude of Rev 7:9:

1. They're not called souls; they have bodies because they are seen wearing their robes, standing and waving palm branches.

2. They seem to arrive in heaven *en masse* and take John by surprise.

3. They have moved from beneath the altar to before the Throne and are in worship and praise.

These two scenes from adjacent chapters of Revelation are completely different in every way. Something of incredible importance must have happened after the sixth seal to create these changes. That something can *only* be a Pre-Wrath rapture.

Anyone who wishes to say otherwise has to be able to explain all of these changes.

Although followers of the Pre-Tribulation rapture theory have felt compelled to respond to such overwhelming proof, they haven't been able to discount the changes occurring after the sixth seal. Consequently, they have attempted to discount a single word found in these verses, one which tells the *source* of the great multitude:

> *Then one of the elders answered, saying to me, "These who are clothed in the white robes, who are they, and where have they come from? I said to him, "My lord, you know." And he said to me, "These are the ones who come out of the great tribulation, and they have washed their robes and made them white in the blood of the Lamb.* **(Rev 7:13-14)**

Before we discuss the Pre-Tribulation argument, Rev 7:13-14 contains yet one more change from the souls of martyrs to the resurrection bodies of the great multitude. When they were under the altar, John knew who they were. But now that the multitude is in resurrection bodies, John *has to ask* who they are. A great change has happened indeed!

The Pre-Tribulation response focuses on the one verse about the great multitude *coming out of the Great Tribulation*. First, some Pre-Tribulation supporters have asked, "Why just those coming out of the Great Tribulation? Why not saints from all the ages?" This misses the point that saints from all the ages *will* come out of the Great Tribulation: They will be resurrected after the sixth seal, when they are included with those raptured into heaven. Saints from all the ages — Daniel, John the Baptist, Paul, etc. —

The Great Multitude

will come out of the Great Tribulation, as *part of* this vast multitude.

Other Pre-Tribulation proponents like to manipulate the tense and meaning of Greek verbs to try and respond. As we have seen in several other articles, they look at the supposed tense of the word *come* in the phrase *who come out of the Great Tribulation* and say, "See, it's present tense. It is an ongoing process. They are coming out of the Great Tribulation one by one."

Just as we have done before, we will again consult Greek linguistic expert Dr. David Mathewson of Denver Seminary. The word *come* this time doesn't even function as a verb. It's part of a participle: *Ones who have come out of the Great Tribulation*. Dr. Mathewson wrote about this particular verse, Rev 7:14, in his *Handbook On the Greek Text*. Speaking of Rev 7:14, Dr. Mathewson wrote:

> *The participle seems to be past in its temporal sphere of reference ... While participles do not indicate time, their relationship to time (past, present, future) can be determined by context.* **Dr. David Mathewson**

Dr. Mathewson says that this particular participle in Rev 7:14 seems to be *past tense*, because the *context* is past tense. And in his book he specifically discredits the idea that this participle should be translated — as some Pre-Tribulation supporters claim — as an ongoing process. Dr. Mathewson mentions two clues about timing that tell him the participle is past tense: First, there is the vision of an already-present group; they are already there, and therefore they arrived in the past. Second, the verb *washed* in the second half of the sentence is past tense, and this verb gives the entire tense-meaning to the participle *ones who come out of the Great Tribulation* as being past tense, as well.

Greek grammar can be difficult. That is why we need to consult contemporary experts. As Dr. Mathewson states, "The great multitude came out of the Great Tribulation previously. It is not an ongoing action." We can confirm this based on Dr. Mathewson's somewhat intricate grammatical analysis, which eliminates the Pre-Tribulation argument.

In conclusion, an enormous change occurred after the opening of the sixth seal. We have detailed the physical changes, but I'd like to give you one last one: A change in *attitude*. At the fifth seal, the souls under the altar cry out to God to begin judging and avenging. However, after the sixth seal, the great multitude does nothing but praise God. Why? Because they were resurrected in the rapture! That rapture happened after the sixth seal, which means there is no Pre-Tribulation, Mid-Tribulation or Post-Tribulation rapture. There can only be a Pre-Wrath rapture.

Article Eighteen

What Direction Do the Elect Go?

When Jesus returns, He will blow the trumpet of God and His angels will gather together the elect:

> *And then He will send forth the angels and will gather together His elect from the four winds, from the farthest end of the earth to the farthest end of heaven.* **(Mark 13:27)**

But where do they go? Pre-Tribulation rapture proponents assume that this is a gathering of Jews and that they are gathered back to the nation of Israel. Post-Tribulation supporters believe this to be the Church, and that believers are gathered into the air to meet Jesus and then return to earth with Him. Followers of the Pre-Wrath theory believe that this is the rapture and that these are the saints being gathered into heaven. Who has it right?

The answer may be right in the text from scripture!

First, we notice that the gathering is a world-wide gathering, from each of the four winds, which can be thought of as the four points of the compass. Second, this gathering will take place from the farthest end of the earth, to the farthest end of heaven. What exactly does this mean? Is the gathering therefore from the earth *up to heaven*? The simple reading of the text implies this, but many — if not most — believe that it means a gathering *from horizon-to-horizon*. The horizon is where the earth and the sky meet.

What Direction Do the Elect Go?

If the passage does mean *horizon-to-horizon*, the choice of wording is certainly unusual. One would normally expect something more along the lines of *from one end of the earth to the other* — not from the end of the earth to the end of heaven. It's a mixed metaphor. Earth-to-heaven would more likely be a vertical gathering, not a horizontal, horizon-to-horizon gathering. This doesn't prove the point, but it certainly infers it.

If we search the Bible, the construct of using both the earth and end of heaven is not found anywhere else. The most common phrase is *end of the earth* or *ends of the earth*, which is found 45 times in scripture. Only in Mark 13 is it used in connection with *the end of heaven*. This unique usage should immediately catch your attention.

Other than Mark 13 and Matt 24, there are only four places in the Bible that refer to the phrase *end of heaven* or *ends of heaven*.

> *Its rising is from one end of the heavens, And its circuit to the other end of them; And there is nothing hidden from its heat.* **(Psm 19:6)**

> *They are coming from a far country, From the farthest horizons, the Lord and His instruments of indignation, to destroy the whole land.* **(Isa 13:5)**

> *I will bring upon Elam the four winds from the four ends of heaven and will scatter them to all these winds; And there will be no nation to which the outcasts of Elam will not go.* **(Jer 49:36)**

> *Indeed, ask now concerning the former days which were before you, since the day that God created man on the earth, and inquire from one end of the heavens to the*

> *other. Has anything been done like this great thing, or has anything been heard like it?* **(Deut 4:32)**

As we see, one passage refers to the path of the sun, and this is either a horizon or outer space. One passage definitely refers to the heavenly abode of God. Then there are two prophetic passages and, depending on their time frame, they either refer to the heavenly abode of God or possibly to a horizon. So, based strictly on Old Testament references, we cannot tell for certain the specific meaning of the phrase *end of heaven*.

However, we must ask the question: Why, out of 50 uses of the phrase *ends of the earth* and *ends of heaven,* is there only one like Mark 13:27 that employs both phrases?

I contend that it is because the passage is discussing something quite different than a gathering from horizon-to-horizon, that it is describing the rapture, *into heaven*.

But there is even more evidence to consider. This phrase has a directional component to it. It uses the Greek preposition *apo*, meaning *away from*. So the gathering is *away from the ends of the earth*. And another Greek preposition, *heros*, completes the directional nature of this phrase, meaning *to or unto*. So the gathering is *away from the ends of the earth to the ends of heaven*.

Most translations give the destination of the saints as the *farthest end of heaven*. What is this? In the first century, the *first heaven* was the atmosphere, the *second heaven* was outer space, and the *third heaven* was the farthest heaven, which was the abode of God. In 2 Cor 2:12, Paul referred to the heavenly abode of God using this exact term, the 3rd heaven:

> *Now when I came to Troas for the gospel of Christ and when a door was opened for me in the Lord.* **(2 Cor 2:12)**

What Direction Do the Elect Go?

Let's look at the nature of this passage in 2 Cor in parallel with the verse we've been examining, Mark 13:27:

1. Both are referring to a rapture. Mark uses the term we've previously discussed, *gathered together,* or *episynagoge.* And Paul uses the same term as 1 Thess., *harpazo,* or *caught* up. Both mean the same thing: Rapture.

2. Both are directional, using the same exact preposition, *heros,* which means *to or unto.*

3. Finally, both end up at the same destination: The farthest end of heaven, or the third heaven.

The Greek term *heros* is a bit of an unusual preposition. Most constructs of this sort use the preposition *eis,* but *heros* carries the meaning that one goes *as far as.* In other words, it implies passing both the first and second heavens to arrive at the destination of the third heaven, thereby gathering as far as the abode of God. So when Paul wrote 2 Cor, was he referring to Mark 13:27 in this use of *heros?* Most likely he was. The constructs are identical, and these are the only two phrases like it in the Bible.

So, to summarize, it is almost certain that Mark 13:27 describes a rapture *into heaven.* First, it's the simple, common sense reading of the text. Second, it's an absolutely unique usage. In 50 plus occurrences of the phrases *end of the earth* and *end of heaven* in the Bible, this is the only one that uses *both* phrases together. Why would the inspired Word of God use this unique construct if it didn't carry a special and unique meaning? And, most importantly, the usage is exactly parallel to 2 Cor 12:2, the only other phrase about a rapture or catching up that specifically mentions it as being into the heavenly abode of God.

In contrast, the Pre-Tribulation rapture theory considers the gathering in Mark 13 to represent a supernatural gathering of Jews back to Israel by angels. But that's not what the Old Testament depicts. Rather, it shows them being gathered by humans and riding horses, mules, and camels:

> *Then they shall bring all your brethren from all the nations as a grain offering to the Lord, on horses, in chariots, in litters, on mules and on camels, to My holy mountain Jerusalem, says the Lord, just as the sons of Israel bring their grain offering in a clean vessel to the house of the Lord.* **(Isa 66:20)**

Isaiah also depicts the Jews returning by boat:

> *Surely the coastlands will wait for Me; And the ships of Tarshish will come first, To bring your sons from afar, Their silver and their gold with them, For the name of the Lord your God, And for the Holy One of Israel because He has glorified you.* **(Isa 60:9)**

But *nowhere* do we see them returning on the wings of angels.

So the question we must ask is this: Why isn't the rapture *into heaven* the accepted view of Mark 13:27? The reason is that it's only consistent with the Pre-Wrath rapture theory, which wasn't expressed until the 1990's. At that point, other theories had spent years popularizing the idea that this verse was discussing a gathering from horizon to horizon. Now, however, you can easily see why this earlier view is highly unlikely. And like all other proofs in this series or articles, an interpretation that favors the Pre-Wrath rapture theory is preferred.

Article Nineteen

Is Matthew 24:31 a Gathering of Christians or Jews?

In this article we're going to quickly disprove the Pre-Tribulation Rapture, and we're going to do it using one of the most currently-popular proofs used by supporters of that theory. This proof comes from a website called *A Little Strength*, by Greg Lauer. If you've seen it, then you know it contends that the gathering together in Matt 24:31 is a gathering of Jews:

> *And he will send out his angels with a loud trumpet call, and they will gather his elect from the four winds, from one end of heaven to the other.* (**Matt 24:31**)

Now, both the Pre-Wrath and Post-Tribulation rapture theories believe this passage is the rapture, so if instead it actually is a gathering together of the Jews, then neither of these rapture theories can be correct. Conversely, if the gathering isn't the Jews, then it can't be a Pre-Tribulation rapture.

So our task is to prove that the gathering in Matt 24 isn't a gathering together of newly saved Jews, which, by the way, will also lead us to demonstrate that the whole notion of dispensationalism may be mistaken, as well. Dispensational theology teaches that there are two distinct peoples of God: Israel and the Church. This is a bit controversial, even among our Prewrath brethren.

Is Matthew 24:31 a Gathering of Christians or Jews?

Now, let's look at Mr. Lauer's point, which is really pretty simple. He compares Matt 24:31 to a number of Old Testament passages about a future gathering of Israel. Here is the first one:

> *In that day from the river Euphrates to the Brook of Egypt the Lord will thresh out the grain, and you will be gleaned one by one, O people of Israel. And in that day a great trumpet will be blown, and those who were lost in the land of Assyria and those who were driven out to the land of Egypt will come and worship the Lord on the holy mountain at Jerusalem.* **(Isa 27:12-13)**

Mr. Lauer points out that there is a gathering, or harvesting, and a trumpet call; and of course, he points out that it is the people of Israel who are being gathered. Mr. Lauer then points out how the rest of Matt 31 quotes other Old Testament passages, as well.

In Zech 2 we learn that God will scatter the Jews to the four winds of heaven:

> *Up! Up! Flee from the land of the north, declares the Lord. For I have spread you abroad as the four winds of the heavens, declares the Lord.* **(Zech 2:6)**

And in Mr. Lauer's opinion, Matt 24:31 is Jesus's explanation of how this re-gathering will take place:

> *And he will send out his angels with a loud trumpet call, and they will gather his elect from the four winds, from one end of heaven to the other.* **(Matt 24:31)**

Mr. Lauer contends that the references to the Old Testament prove that it is the Jews who will be re-gathered, and that it is not a rapture. In Mr. Lauer's mind, this disproves both the Pre-Wrath and Post-Tribulation rapture positions.

This proof has convinced a lot of people. And guess what — even I agree with Mr. Lauer that Jesus was quoting the Old Testament in Matt 24:31. I just don't agree with his conclusions.

The first thing Mr. Lauer misses is that believers in the Messiah now include — and have included for nearly two thousand years — many who are Jewish by birth. Paul, Peter, John, etc. were all Jewish, as are many of my Christian brothers and friends today. So when Isaiah says God will gather Israel at the great trumpet, He will! On the day of the resurrection and rapture, many genetic Jews will be believers and will be raised and raptured.

Second, when God's Word refers to Israel, it sometimes refers to the nation, the genetic Jews, and sometimes it refers to a greater group — the Israel of God.

Mr. Lauer and most Pre-Tribulation followers believe that God has two distinct sets of people — the Jews and the Christians. These people believe that after the crucifixion God stopped working with the Jews and began dealing solely with the Christians. Further, they believe that when the Tribulation finally begins, God will take the Christians out of this world in the rapture and begin dealing only with the Jews, to finally bring them to faith in Jesus. This is the basic idea behind dispensationalism. To many, this sounds correct. It has a nice feel to it. But the truth is, it's totally unbiblical. God has only one people on earth — and they are neither Jew nor Gentile. We are all one people in Jesus:

> *There is neither Jew nor Greek, there is neither slave nor free, there is no male and female, for you are all one in Christ Jesus.* **(Gal 3:28)**

Is Matthew 24:31 a Gathering of Christians or Jews?

The Apostle Paul describes God's people as a single olive tree, which is the Israel of God. Not the nation of Israel or those who are genetic Israel, but the spiritual inhabitants of the New Jerusalem. What about gentile Christians? Paul tells us that although we aren't Jewish by birth, we were grafted into the root of the tree, which is spiritual Israel. By becoming Christians, we became part of *true* Spiritual Israel. This is a critical truth that is rarely taught:

> *You, although a wild olive shoot, were grafted in among the others and now share in the nourishing root of the olive tree.* **(Rom 11:17)**

And what is that *nourishing root*? Paul tells us in Romans, as well:

> *Israelites, to whom belongs the adoption as sons, and the glory and the covenants and the giving of the Law and the temple service and the promises, whose are the fathers, and from whom is the Christ according to the flesh.* **(Rom 9:4-5)**

So to the Israel of God belongs the adoption as sons, our coming glorification, the covenants, the Law, the promises of scripture, and our Messiah Himself. That is what we were grafted into.

Paul additionally says this in Ephesians:

> *You were at that time separate from Christ, excluded from the commonwealth of Israel, and strangers to the covenants of promise, having no hope and without God in the world. But now in Christ Jesus you who formerly were far off have been brought near by the blood of Christ.* **(Eph 2:12-13)**

There is something called the *commonwealth of Israel* to which Gentile Christians were brought near by the blood of Jesus. Paul calls this the Israel of God in Galatians:

> *For neither is circumcision anything, nor uncircumcision, but a new creation. And those who will walk by this rule, peace and mercy be upon them, and upon the Israel of God.* **(Gal 6:15-16)**

The Israel of God is a new creation — neither Jew nor Greek — whose capital is the New Jerusalem. But what about the *unsaved Jews*?

Their branches were *broken off* because of their unbelief, so they *aren't currently part of true Israel*. They are genetically Israel and part of the nation of Israel, but not *true* Israel. This seems a contradiction and unbelievable, but that is what the Bible teaches:

> *They were broken off because of their unbelief.* **(Rom 11:20)**

So, God has only one people on the earth — a single olive tree. The unsaved Jews have been cut off for their unbelief, but God has a plan to *re-graft* them some day. This is critical, because God made promises to the genetic descendants of Jacob. And He will fulfill them:

> *A partial hardening has happened to Israel until the fullness of the Gentiles has come in; and so all Israel will be saved ... From the standpoint of the gospel they are enemies for your sake, but from the standpoint of God's choice they are beloved for the sake of the fathers; for the gifts and the calling of God are irrevocable.* **(Rom 11:25-26, 28-29)**

Is Matthew 24:31 a Gathering of Christians or Jews?

But what does all this have to do with the gathering together in Matt 24? Because of their dispensational beliefs, Mr. Lauer and most Pre-Tribulation followers make a very faulty assumption, which is that Old Testament scriptures — like the ones quoted here — are only for the unsaved Jews. This is so wrong! The Church is part of the Israel of God, the one *true* Israel, into which they were grafted, and into which the unsaved Jews will be grafted back some day.

Let's look more closely at why this dispensational approach is faulty thinking. The New Covenant that Jesus said was in His blood at the Last Supper — the same Covenant that Christians currently believe applies to us — was made with the houses of Judah and Israel, not with Christians:

> *Behold, the days are coming, declares the Lord, when I will make a new covenant with the house of Israel and the house of Judah.* **(Jer 31:31)**

So how does this Covenant apply to us today? It applies to Christians because we were grafted into the Israel of God and therefore became recipients of the same benefits, in the same way, as depicted by various Old Testament passages, like the ones Mr. Lauer references. When Jesus taught Matt 24, He took many of these Old Testament prophecies and put them together like a jigsaw puzzle, so that His disciples and those of us who came later could know how they all fit together. But — and this is crucially important — there was no Church yet. No one had been grafted back at that point.

So when Mr. Lauer makes his so-called proof, he only looks at half the story. He stopped with Jesus's explanation. But there is one more critical explanation. It took the Apostle Paul to explain to us how Christians fit into the picture Jesus painted.

When Paul wrote to the Gentile believers in Thessalonica, he told them that they would be part of this gathering together that Jesus described. He told them Jesus would descend from heaven, resurrect the dead in Christ, and the living and dead would be gathered together to meet the Lord in the air. This is Paul's explanation of how Matt 24:31 applies to Christians:

> *For the Lord Himself will descend from heaven with a cry of command, with the voice of an archangel, and with the sound of the trumpet of God. And the dead in Christ will rise first. Then we who are alive, who are left, will be caught up together with them in the clouds to meet the Lord in the air, and so we will always be with the Lord.* **(1 Thess 4:16-17)**

You may be saying, "Wait a minute. What you're reading about in 1 Thess is the rapture. Jesus was describing the Second Coming in Matt 24:31." But that's just wrong — 1 Thess. and Matt 24 are exactly the same event! They are both the rapture, and we have already proven that in a separate Article 11, which is entitled, *Is Matthew 24:31 The Rapture or The Second Coming?*

Now, with respect to the *gathering together*, there were three teachings:

1. Isaiah taught that Israel would be gathered at a great trumpet, and at that point in time it looked like this would just be the Jews. **(Isa 27:12-13)**

2. Then Jesus placed the piece of the puzzle in the chronology of the end times that told us the gathering together happens after the Great Tribulation. **(Matt 24:31)**

Is Matthew 24:31 a Gathering of Christians or Jews?

3. But it took the Apostle Paul to show that the gathering of true Israel, the one and only olive tree, is actually the rapture of Christians. **(1 Thess 4:16-17)**

In fact, all three of these teachings are of the same event.

Now let me share a couple of bonus facts about the gathering together. The unsaved Jews will eventually be grafted back into the olive tree and will be re-gathered to the nation of Israel. But the gathering of Jews won't happen supernaturally with the help of angels. As we have discussed previously, after the return of Jesus, Jews will return to their homeland by way of camel, horse, mule, and boat. As Isaiah tells us:

> *And they shall bring all your brothers from all the nations as an offering to the Lord, on horses and in chariots and in litters and on mules and on dromedaries, to my holy mountain Jerusalem.* **(Isa 66:20)**

> *The ships of Tarshish first, to bring your children from afar.* **(Isa 60:9)**

So, the gathering together by angels in Matt 24 can't be the *Jews*, because the Bible asserts that their *gathering will be by natural means.* Plus, there is the small matter that those who are gathered are called the *elect*!

Our discussion of the Pre-Tribulation proof that everyone has been so excited about actually has helped us to uncover a number of facts:

1. That God has *one people* on the earth, not two: One true Israel, and all Christians have been grafted into it. This is our true identity.

2. Shockingly, Matt 24:31 and the most universally-accepted passage on the rapture, 1 Thess 4, are the same event, the rapture.

3. God will re-gather Israel by using physical means like horses and camels, not by using angels.

4. The *elect* in Matt 24 are Christians, not newly-saved Jews.

And finally — as Mr. Lauer himself tells us— if the re-gathering of Matt 24 isn't of the Jews, then it must be the rapture. And since we've clearly shown that it isn't the Jews, we have also proven that there isn't a Pre-Tribulation rapture. There can only be a Pre-Wrath rapture.

Article Twenty

Is the Great Tribulation Cut Short?

It's almost a foregone conclusion of most Christians that the Great Tribulation is a full three-and-a-half years long. Yet scripture seems to tell us that those days are *cut short*. We will examine this issue in this article.

Jesus tells us that immediately after the abomination of desolation there will be great tribulation:

> *For then there will be a great tribulation, such as has not occurred since the beginning of the world until now, nor ever will.* **(Matt 24:21)**

Notice that Jesus tells us there will be great tribulation, not that there will be *a Great Tribulation*, or that it will last any specific length of time. In fact, in the very next verse Jesus tells us the days of great tribulation will be cut short:

> *Unless those days had been cut short, no life would have been saved; but for the sake of the elect those days will be cut short.* **(Matt 24:22)**

Now, the common-sense, straightforward reading of the text imagines that it will be less than three-and-a-half years. The Greek word translated *cut short* literally means to amputate, and it is used that way in the Septuagint Old Testament and in Greek literature by Aristotle, Theodorus, and Polybius, among others. So the days of what we call the *Great Tribulation* will be amputated from their proposed length.

Is the Great Tribulation Cut Short?

Daniel the prophet told us what the decreed number of days would be:

> *He will speak out against the Most High and wear down the saints of the Highest One, and he will intend to make alterations in times and in law; and they will be given into his hand for a time, times, and half a time.* **(Dan 7:25)**

Those days would be *time times and half a time*, or what most scholars believe to be 1,260 days. So those days that Jesus mentioned in Matt 24:22 are the 1,260 days. They are the ones cut short or amputated. The Great Tribulation will therefore be less than the 1,260 days of the second half of the 70th Week of Daniel.

All of us know that God's Word cannot be broken. So how is it that Daniel can tell us that the Great Tribulation will be 1,260 days, and yet Jesus can tell us that those days are shortened? The answer is actually much simpler than you think!

First of all, Daniel doesn't call this period the Great Tribulation. He doesn't give it a name at all. Let's look at the passage again:

> *He will speak out against the Most High and wear down the saints of the Highest One, and he will intend to make alterations in times and in law; and they will be given into his hand for a time, times, and half a time.* **(Dan 7:25)**

He simply says that the Antichrist will *wear down* the saints, and that they shall be given into his hands for a period of 1,260 days. The saints are both Jews and Christians, and both will be oppressed by the Antichrist. Jews will be oppressed for the entire period, but Christians won't be. Notice Jesus tells us that for the sake of the *elect* Christians — and only for the elect — those days will be shortened.

This of course fits perfectly with the Pre-Wrath rapture position, which holds that the Great Tribulation only lasts a portion of the last half of the Tribulation period. Then the rapture takes place, which cuts the Tribulation short for Christians who are raptured into heaven. This cutting short for the *elect only* is exactly what Jesus described in Matt 24.

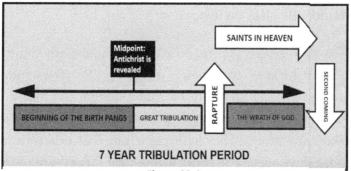

Figure 20-1

But the Antichrist and his armies will continue to persecute and kill the Jews right up until the final return of Jesus. In this way, Dan 7:25 will be fulfilled. The Antichrist will *wear out* God's unsaved Jewish people for the full 1,260 days. Thus, both Matt 24:22 and Dan 7:25 will be fulfilled perfectly, and God's Word will not be broken.

What cuts the Great Tribulation short? Jesus tells us directly only a few verses later:

Is the Great Tribulation Cut Short?

> *But immediately after the tribulation of those days the sun will be darkened, and the moon will not give its light, and the stars will fall from the sky, and the powers of the heavens will be shaken.* **(Matt 24:9)**

Those days of the Tribulation will be cut short at the sixth seal by the darkening of the sun and moon. And the sixth seal happens long before — maybe even a year before — the end of the Tribulation period. So the Great Tribulation can't be the entire three-and-a-half years of the second half, can it? No, it's impossible, because it's cut short by the sixth seal! What can Pre-Tribulation supporters say in defense of that? God's Word is so abundantly clear on this point!

But, as we have seen before, when confronted with significant evidence contrary to their position, Pre-Tribulationists frequently challenge scripture by manipulating the meaning of Greek terms — in this case, the verb translated as *cut short* that we looked at earlier. They will point out that this translation says those days were cut short in the past. They will contend that this isn't a future cutting-short, but, rather, one that has already happened. Their incorrect claim is that the Antichrist intends to continue the Great Tribulation until all Jews and Christians are killed. But in Dan 7:25 it was God who decreed that the Great Tribulation would be cut short, to *only* 1,260 days from some indefinite period. So it was a *historic* cutting-short.

This sounds good, until you examine things more closely. The verb translated *cut short* — *koloboo*, meaning *to amputate* — is in the *aorist* tense, a Greek tense not found in the English language. So we will once again return to the expert testimony of Dr. David Mathewson of Denver Seminary. As we mentioned in an earlier article, Dr. Mathewson tells us that the *aorist* tense can assume past, present, or future tense meanings, depending on the context of the word. So maybe the word translated *cut short* isn't in the past at all.

If we look closely at this verse, we do in fact find that there are two verbs in the *aorist* tense. The first one is *cut short*, and the second one is the verb *saved*. If the cutting short happened long ago, then so did the *saving*. But no one believes that. The saving is obviously in the future. And if the saving is in the future, well, then so is the cutting-short. The two *aorist* verbs must coincide and agree.

And if that isn't enough, there's more evidence that confirms our position completely. Although both of these verbs are in the *aorist* tense, there is yet another verb in this verse that isn't. It's in the *future* tense: *Will be cut short*. And the tense of this final verb gives the entire sentence it's time context! The cutting-short and the saving will be in the future, not in the past.

In summary, we can be sure that the Great Tribulation is less than three-and-a-half years long. It is the common-sense, straightforward reading of scripture. The Great Tribulation is cut short by the sixth seal, which occurs long before the end of the second half of Daniels 70th Week. And finally, this interpretation is consistent with Greek grammar. *Only* the Pre-Wrath rapture envisions a Great Tribulation that is cut short, consistent with all of scripture.

Article Twenty One

Only 5 Wise Virgins?

> *Enter through the narrow gate; for the gate is wide and the way is broad that leads to destruction, and there are many who enter through it. For the gate is small and the way is narrow that leads to life, and there are few who find it.* **(Matt 7:13-14)**

There are over 2 billion self-professed Christians worldwide. Sixty-two percent of all Americans belong to church congregations. Does this sound like a few? Does this give the impression of a narrow gate or road to you? To me it sounds like many who think they are saved, but really are not.

Jesus's parables appear to have come to a similar conclusion. In the parable of the wheat and the tares, the field is covered with both wheat and weeds. The actual type of weed that Jesus mentions is *zizania*. This plant looks just like wheat, but it never forms any grain. So the weeds Jesus taught about that would be cast into fire were not those that were actively opposed to His Gospel; rather, it was those that look just like real Christians, but never produce any fruit.

In the parable of the sower, seed is cast into four types of soil. Those with hearts like rocky soil initially receive the Gospel with joy. They attend church, they look and act like Christians. They may even think they are Christians — until the Word tells us that persecution arises and they fall away:

> *The one on whom seed was sown on the rocky places, this is the man who hears the word and immediately receives it with joy; yet he has no firm root in himself, but is only temporary, and when affliction or persecution arises because of the word, immediately he falls away.* **(Matt 13:20-21)**

So someone can receive the Gospel, look like a true believer, think they are a true believer, and yet not be saved. And notice in this case that it is persecution — just like that of the Great Tribulation — that causes them to fall away.

In the parable of the ten virgins, all of the virgins are anxiously awaiting the return of the bridegroom; but only five enter the wedding feast. As we've mentioned several times in this book, all ten are virgins, people trying hard to keep themselves pure for the bridegroom, people who think they're going to be taken into the wedding feast. But by this parable, scripture is clear that some 50 percent of them will have the door of heaven closed to them.

In this article we will examine this seminal parable in more detail and consider what we might do as churches and individuals with the lessons that it teaches. Because understanding rapture theory isn't enough. God's Word is given to us to apply. We must be *doers* of the Word:

> *But prove yourselves doers of the word, and not merely hearers who delude themselves.* **(Jas 1:22)**

One of the things we learn from this parable is that *all* of those waiting for the bridegroom fall asleep. This is indicative of us not knowing the timing of Jesus's return:

> *Now while the bridegroom was delaying, they all got drowsy and began to sleep.* **(Matt 25:5)**

Right now, none of us know when Jesus will return. Like the virgins, all of us are sleeping. But in the parable, something happens at midnight, the darkest hour. A shout goes out that the bridegroom is coming. All of the virgins are alerted that the bridegroom will soon be there.

Now, many have mistakenly thought that this is the same shout and voice of the archangel that accompanies Jesus's descent from heaven in 1 Thess 4:16. But it isn't.

All of the virgins have time to light their lamps. The lamps of the foolish burned for a while, but then go out. But even then, time remains for the foolish virgins to run off to buy more oil. That's a lot of time. This event isn't the shout at Jesus's return. It's a warning sign. Earlier, we learned what that warning sign will be:

> *Therefore when you see the Abomination of Desolation which was spoken of through Daniel the prophet, standing in the holy place ... For then there will be a great tribulation, such as has not occurred since the beginning of the world until now, nor ever will.* **(Matt 24:15, 21)**

It's the abomination of desolation, the one sign that all Christians need to be aware of and recognize. Because immediately afterward, the Great Tribulation will begin. And what are the lamps that the virgin's all lighted? Although most English translations say *lamps,* the Greek term is actually *lampas,* the word for torches. It is the very same term used to describe the torches that Gideon and his army used against the Midianites in the book of Joshua, and just like the seven torches before God's Throne in Rev 4. So these are very bright lights, indeed!

> *And I saw the souls of those who had been beheaded because of their testimony of Jesus and because of the word of God* (**Rev 20:4**)

What do these torches stand for? Probably a person's *testimony of Jesus*. The term *testimony of the saints* is mentioned nine separate times in the book of Revelation.

In the parable, the foolish virgins don't have enough oil for their torches, and the torches go out. What is the oil? Most likely it is the Holy Spirit. The unsaved don't have the Holy Spirit. And in the end times — with the deception and persecution by Antichrist — *only* those who have the Holy Spirit, *the elect*, will have sufficient oil to overcome. Everyone else will fall away.

Late in the parable we read what surely is one of the saddest passages in the Bible: *The door was shut.* The door of heaven was shut to the foolish virgins. And although they cry out to Jesus to open it, He says that He does not know them. They know Him, but not vice- versa. This is a parallel to a prophecy which Jesus spoke during the Sermon on the Mount:

> *Many will say to Me on that day, 'Lord, Lord, did we not prophesy in Your name, and in Your name cast out demons, and in Your name perform many miracles? And then I will declare to them, 'I never knew you; Depart from me, you who practice lawlessness.'* (**Matt 7:22-23**)

In this parable, church-goers cast out demons in the name of Jesus and perform many miracles. They believe they are Christians. But they are the same as the foolish virgins of Matt 25. And Jesus's answer is the same, as well: Although they think they are Christians, He doesn't know them.

So returning to the parable of the ten virgins, we find that Jesus is telling us that 50 percent of those who think they are Christians at the time of the abomination of desolation will fall away, due to persecution and deception. They will not be raptured into heaven. Not only that, Jesus is telling us in this parable that if you aren't saved at the moment of the abomination, the deception and persecution of the Great Tribulation will occur so quickly and severely that there may not be time to buy oil. Those who are not prepared may well not be saved.

Clearly our churches — and their millions of Christians — are at great risk. Most are doing nothing about it. Absolutely nothing. What should they be doing? Well, primarily they should be teaching their church-goers that the coming generation may well face the Antichrist. As it is, a large number of Christians will enter the end times blindfolded to the truth.

On the night He was betrayed, Jesus pleaded with His disciples to watch and pray. Instead, just like the foolish virgins, they fell asleep. By the time they woke up, Judas, the first son of destruction, was already upon them. Without time to prepare themselves emotionally to stand with Jesus, and without the strengthening power of prayer, their fear caused them to run away and abandon Jesus.

The foolish virgins who make up 50 percent of those in our church pews are currently sleeping. Jesus is pleading with them to watch and pray, as well. But they are going on with their lives, as if facing the Antichrist isn't even a possibility. Collectively, we must pray for the Holy Spirit to touch the hearts of those who would otherwise become the foolish. We must share what we know with others. Above all, we must encourage the study of scripture and the pursuit of God's saving truth.

Made in the USA
Monee, IL
21 December 2022